SPOTTER'S HANDBOOK

Flowers, Trees and Birds of North America

Michael Ruggiero, Alan Mitchell
and Philip Burton

Part 1 (Wild Flowers): Consultant:
Michael A. Ruggiero. Illustrated by Joyce Bee.
Part 2 (Trees): Consultants:
Alan Mitchell and Michael A. Ruggiero.
Illustrated by Peter Stebbing and Annabel Milne.
Part 3 (Birds): Consultants:
Dr Philip Burton and Dr Kenneth Cooper.
Illustrated by Trevor Boyer
and Tim Hayward.

MAYFLOWER BOOKS
NEW YORK

Contents

Manufactured in Spain by Printer, industria gráfica sa Sant Vicenç dels Horts, Barcelona
D.L. 14.145-1979

Edited by Karen Goaman.

Library of Congress Cataloging in Publication Data

Ruggiero, Michael. 1946
The spotter's handbook.

1. Wild flowers – North America – Identification.
2. Trees – North America – Identification.
3. Birds – North America – Identification.
I. Mitchell, Alan F., joint author. II. Burton, Philip John Kennedy. III. Title.
QL681.R83   582'.097   79-10397
ISBN 0-8317-7953-5
ISBN 0-8317-7954-3 pbk.

First American Edition

The material in this book is also available as three separate books: Wild Flowers, Trees, and Birds, in the Spotter's Guides series, published by Mayflower Books, Inc.

Part 1 Wild flowers

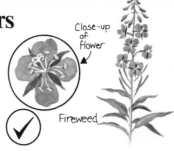

Close-up of Flower

Fireweed

This section of the book contains an identification guide to some of the wild flowers of North America.

The flowers are arranged by color – yellow flowers first, followed by orange, pink, red or red-purple, blue or blue-purple and lastly white flowers. Remember that some flowers can be two or more colors.

The pictures in circles next to the main illustrations show close-ups of flowers, or a plant's fruits or seeds. These will help you to identify the plant. For example, the picture in the circle beside the illustration of the Fireweed shows a close-up of a single flower.

The description next to each flower will also help you to identify it. The plants are not drawn to scale, but the description gives you the range of their height, measured from the ground. If the plant has a climbing, creeping or trailing stem, the length of its stem is given rather than the height. The description also tells you when the plant flowers. Beside the description is a small blank circle. Each time you see a flower, check it off in the circle.

The names of flowers

Many flowers have more than one common name and may be known by different names in different parts of North America. Only one common name appears in the description of each flower, but some other commonly used names appear on page 62.

Each plant has a Latin name which remains the same everywhere, and a list of these appears on pages 63-64. The Latin name is useful to know for further study.

Scorecard

The scorecard on pages 58-62 gives you scores for each flower shown in the book. There are separate scores for different areas of North America: look at the map on page 58 to find out which area you are in.

You can also use the scorecard to find out the areas in which a flower grows, and how common or rare it is in each area: a very common plant scores 5 and a very rare or interesting one scores 25.

What to take

Take this book, plus a notebook and pencils, and a camera, if you have one, so that you can record the flowers you find by drawing or photographing them and making notes. See page 55 for hints on how to do this. Take a tape measure to measure the height of plants and the length of runners. A hand lens will help you to take a closer look at the parts of flower heads (see page 49 for the names of the main parts of a flower).

If you find a flower that is not in this book, your drawing and notes will help you to identify it from other books later. There is a list of useful books on page 57.

Yellow Adder's-tongue ▶

Flowering plant has two leaves mottled with maroon; young plant has one. Usually in large groups in woods. 2-8″ tall. Spring.

Flowers often spotted near base

◀ Yellow Lady's-slipper

Up to six pointed leaves and one or two fragrant flowers. Bogs, marshes and dry to moist woods. 6-28″ tall. From spring to early summer.

Swamp Buttercup ▶

Deeply divided leaves on trailing stems. Look on banks of streams, in woods and meadows. Stems 12-36″ long. From spring to early summer.

4

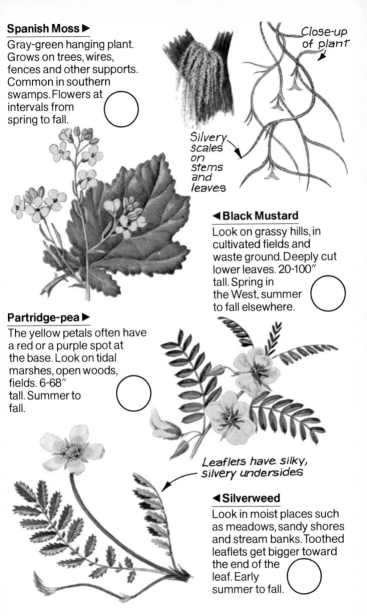

Spanish Moss ▶

Gray-green hanging plant.
Grows on trees, wires,
fences and other supports.
Common in southern
swamps. Flowers at
intervals from
spring to fall.

Close-up of plant

Silvery scales on stems and leaves

◀ Black Mustard

Look on grassy hills, in
cultivated fields and
waste ground. Deeply cut
lower leaves. 20-100"
tall. Spring in
the West, summer
to fall elsewhere.

Partridge-pea ▶

The yellow petals often have
a red or a purple spot at
the base. Look on tidal
marshes, open woods,
fields. 6-68"
tall. Summer to
fall.

Leaflets have silky, silvery undersides

◀ Silverweed

Look in moist places such
as meadows, sandy shores
and stream banks. Toothed
leaflets get bigger toward
the end of the
leaf. Early
summer to fall.

5

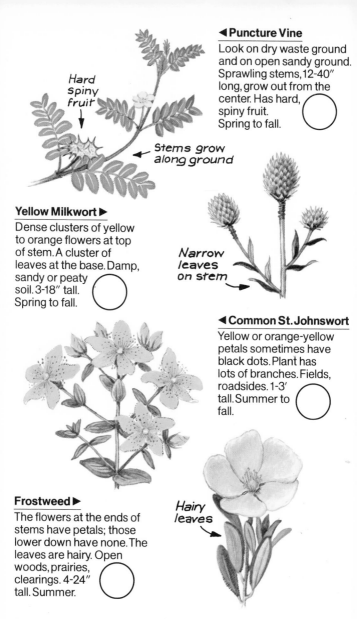

◄ Puncture Vine
Look on dry waste ground and on open sandy ground. Sprawling stems, 12-40" long, grow out from the center. Has hard, spiny fruit. Spring to fall.

Hard spiny fruit

Stems grow along ground

Yellow Milkwort ►
Dense clusters of yellow to orange flowers at top of stem. A cluster of leaves at the base. Damp, sandy or peaty soil. 3-18" tall. Spring to fall.

Narrow leaves on stem

◄ Common St. Johnswort
Yellow or orange-yellow petals sometimes have black dots. Plant has lots of branches. Fields, roadsides. 1-3' tall. Summer to fall.

Frostweed ►
The flowers at the ends of stems have petals; those lower down have none. The leaves are hairy. Open woods, prairies, clearings. 4-24" tall. Summer.

Hairy leaves

Downy Yellow Violet ▶

Look in woods for yellow flowers with purple veins. Stems and leaves have fine hairs. Leaves are heart shaped. Stem 4-18″ long. Spring.

Often has reddish-colored stem

◀ Common Evening-primrose

Yellow flowers open near sunset. Waste ground, woods in the East; along streams and in meadows in the West. 6-80″ tall. Summer to fall.

Greater Bladderwort ▶

Floats freely just below surface of quiet waters. Flower stems are 4-32″ tall and grow above water. Leaflets are threadlike. Spring to fall.

Close-up of flower

Sacs (bladders) trap tiny animals for food

Leaflets

Close-up of flower

◀ Common Mullein

A sturdy plant covered in grayish or brownish down. Look in fields, woods, waste ground, or on rocky banks. Up to 6′ tall. Spring to fall.

Flowers grow in clusters on club shaped head

7

Flowers curve downward at tip

Wood-betony ◄
Dense clusters of yellow or red flowers at ends of clustered unbranched stems. 6-16" tall. Look in spring in meadows, woods, prairies and clearings.

Common Monkey-flower ►
Yellow flowers usually spotted red. Leaves are broad and toothed. Stem usually branched. Look in wet places from spring to fall. Stem 2-40" tall.

Stamens

Yellow Blazing-star ◄
Flowers open toward the evening. Yellow, narrow petals. Lots of stamens. Look in deserts and other sandy places. 8-60" tall. Summer to fall.

Buffalo-gourd ►
Leaves have an unpleasant smell. Trailing stems are up to 20' long. Gravelly or sandy soil in scrub, grassland, roadsides. Spring to summer.

Fruit

Yellow Sand-verbena ▶

Look in sandy places by
the coast. Flowers grow
on short stalks in
rounded clusters. Sticky,
spreading stems
12-40″ long.
Spring to fall.

*Thick
leaves
on long
stalks*

*Rough,
hairy
stems
and
leaves*

◀ Black-eyed Susan

Flower heads have dark
brown centers and many
orange-yellow or yellow
petals. Found in fields
and woods. 12-40″
tall. Spring
to summer.

Common Sunflower ▶

Broad, hairy leaves and
large flower heads. Grows
in fields, waste ground
and on roadsides. Summer
(spring in West)
to fall.
8-13′ tall.

◀ Blanket-flower

Petals usually red with
yellow tips; sometimes
purple, or purple tipped
with yellow. Sandy places.
8-24″ tall.
Late spring to
summer.

9

Fruits have parachutes

◄ Common Dandelion

Plant has a milky sap. Naked flower stalks, each topped by one flower head. Leaves grow in a rosette. Look on open ground. Up to 8″ tall. Spring to fall.

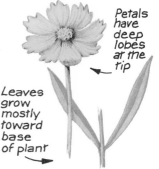

Petals have deep lobes at the tip

Leaves grow mostly toward base of plant

Tickseed ►

Yellow flower heads have long stalks. Leaves are narrow. Look in dry gravelly, rocky and/or sandy places. 8-32″ tall. Spring to summer.

◄ Goldenrod

Look in thickets and in moist open places. Small flower heads are borne in dense clusters. Plant is usually smooth. 20-100″ tall. Summer to fall.

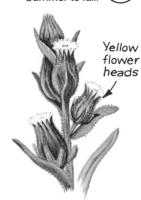

Yellow flower heads

Gumweed ►

Hairy plant has yellow flower heads. Narrow leaves smell of resin. Look in open places, on wooded hillsides. 4-40″ tall. Spring to summer.

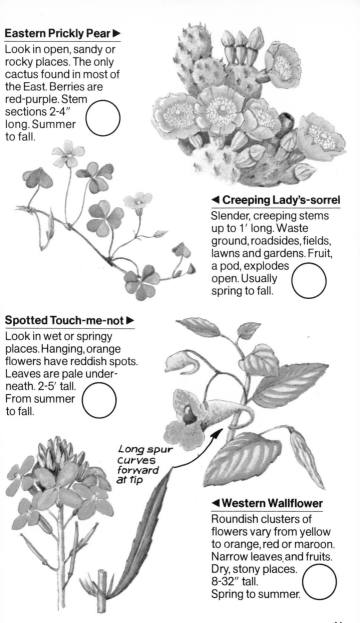

Eastern Prickly Pear ▶

Look in open, sandy or rocky places. The only cactus found in most of the East. Berries are red-purple. Stem sections 2-4" long. Summer to fall.

◀ Creeping Lady's-sorrel

Slender, creeping stems up to 1' long. Waste ground, roadsides, fields, lawns and gardens. Fruit, a pod, explodes open. Usually spring to fall.

Spotted Touch-me-not ▶

Look in wet or springy places. Hanging, orange flowers have reddish spots. Leaves are pale underneath. 2-5' tall. From summer to fall.

Long spur curves forward at tip

◀ Western Wallflower

Roundish clusters of flowers vary from yellow to orange, red or maroon. Narrow leaves and fruits. Dry, stony places. 8-32" tall. Spring to summer.

11

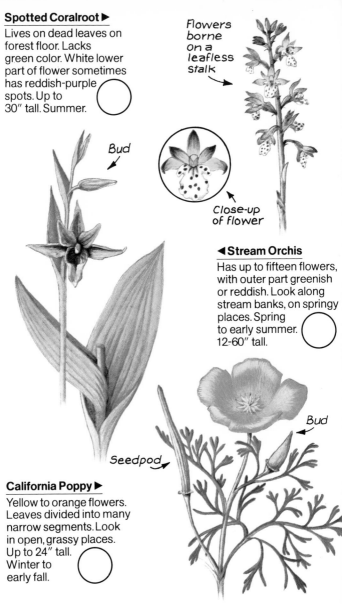

Spotted Coralroot ▶
Lives on dead leaves on forest floor. Lacks green color. White lower part of flower sometimes has reddish-purple spots. Up to 30" tall. Summer.

Flowers borne on a leafless stalk

Bud

Close-up of flower

◀ Stream Orchis
Has up to fifteen flowers, with outer part greenish or reddish. Look along stream banks, on springy places. Spring to early summer. 12-60" tall.

Bud

Seedpod

California Poppy ▶
Yellow to orange flowers. Leaves divided into many narrow segments. Look in open, grassy places. Up to 24" tall. Winter to early fall.

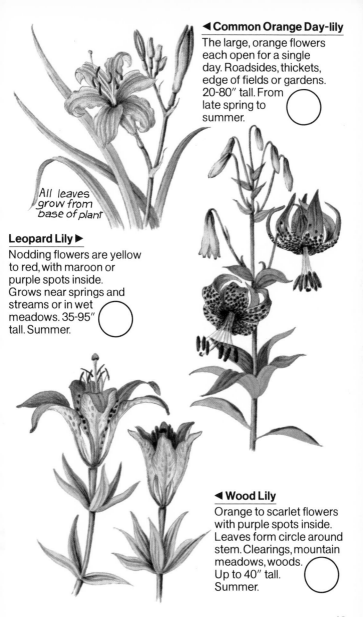

◀ Common Orange Day-lily

The large, orange flowers each open for a single day. Roadsides, thickets, edge of fields or gardens. 20-80″ tall. From late spring to summer.

All leaves grow from base of plant

Leopard Lily ▶

Nodding flowers are yellow to red, with maroon or purple spots inside. Grows near springs and streams or in wet meadows. 35-95″ tall. Summer.

◀ Wood Lily

Orange to scarlet flowers with purple spots inside. Leaves form circle around stem. Clearings, mountain meadows, woods. Up to 40″ tall. Summer.

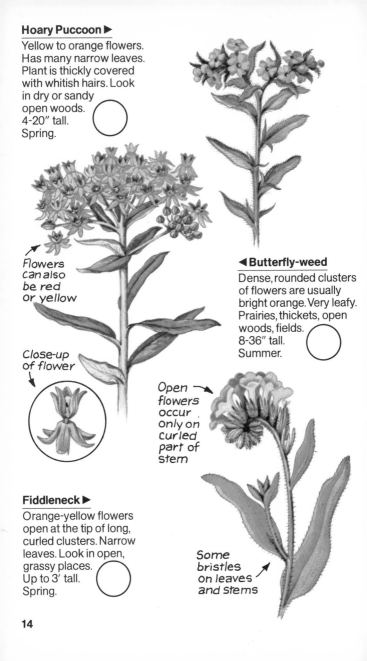

Hoary Puccoon ▶

Yellow to orange flowers. Has many narrow leaves. Plant is thickly covered with whitish hairs. Look in dry or sandy open woods. 4-20" tall. Spring.

Flowers can also be red or yellow

Close-up of flower

◀ Butterfly-weed

Dense, rounded clusters of flowers are usually bright orange. Very leafy. Prairies, thickets, open woods, fields. 8-36" tall. Summer.

Open flowers occur only on curled part of stem

Fiddleneck ▶

Orange-yellow flowers open at the tip of long, curled clusters. Narrow leaves. Look in open, grassy places. Up to 3' tall. Spring.

Some bristles on leaves and stems

14

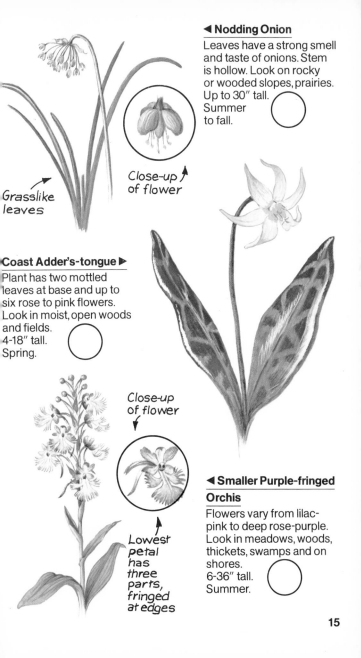

◀ Nodding Onion

Leaves have a strong smell and taste of onions. Stem is hollow. Look on rocky or wooded slopes, prairies. Up to 30" tall. Summer to fall.

Grasslike leaves

Close-up of flower

Coast Adder's-tongue ▶

Plant has two mottled leaves at base and up to six rose to pink flowers. Look in moist, open woods and fields. 4-18" tall. Spring.

Close-up of flower

Lowest petal has three parts, fringed at edges

◀ Smaller Purple-fringed Orchis

Flowers vary from lilac-pink to deep rose-purple. Look in meadows, woods, thickets, swamps and on shores. 6-36" tall. Summer.

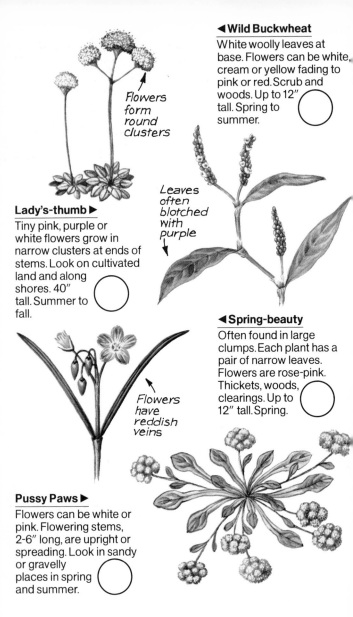

Flowers form round clusters

◀ Wild Buckwheat
White woolly leaves at base. Flowers can be white, cream or yellow fading to pink or red. Scrub and woods. Up to 12" tall. Spring to summer.

Lady's-thumb ▶
Tiny pink, purple or white flowers grow in narrow clusters at ends of stems. Look on cultivated land and along shores. 40" tall. Summer to fall.

Leaves often blotched with purple

◀ Spring-beauty
Often found in large clumps. Each plant has a pair of narrow leaves. Flowers are rose-pink. Thickets, woods, clearings. Up to 12" tall. Spring.

Flowers have reddish veins

Pussy Paws ▶
Flowers can be white or pink. Flowering stems, 2-6" long, are upright or spreading. Look in sandy or gravelly places in spring and summer.

Bitter Root ▶

Rose-pink or white flower has about fifteen petals. Flowering stem ¾" long. Fleshy leaves at base. Look in rocky mountain places. Spring to summer.

Toothed petal has pale spots near base

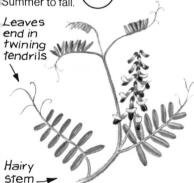

Close-up of flower

◀ Deptford Pink

Upright plant with very narrow leaves. Small pink to red flowers. Found in fields and along roadsides. Up to 32" tall. Late spring to summer.

Bouncing Bet ▶

Pink or white flowers. Leaves contain soaplike substance. Found in fields, roadsides, waste ground, railroad banks. 36" tall. Summer to fall.

Leaves end in twining tendrils

Hairy stem ➜

◀ Hairy Vetch

Top petal of flower is white, the rest usually violet. Trailing or climbing stems are 20-40" long. Fields and roadsides. From spring to fall.

17

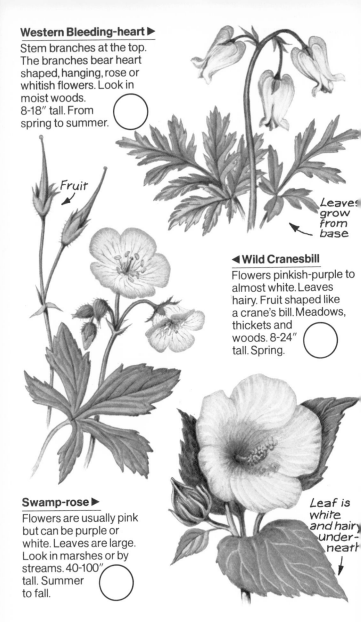

Western Bleeding-heart ▶
Stem branches at the top. The branches bear heart shaped, hanging, rose or whitish flowers. Look in moist woods. 8-18" tall. From spring to summer.

Fruit

Leaves grow from base

◀ Wild Cranesbill
Flowers pinkish-purple to almost white. Leaves hairy. Fruit shaped like a crane's bill. Meadows, thickets and woods. 8-24" tall. Spring.

Swamp-rose ▶
Flowers are usually pink but can be purple or white. Leaves are large. Look in marshes or by streams. 40-100" tall. Summer to fall.

Leaf is white and hairy underneath

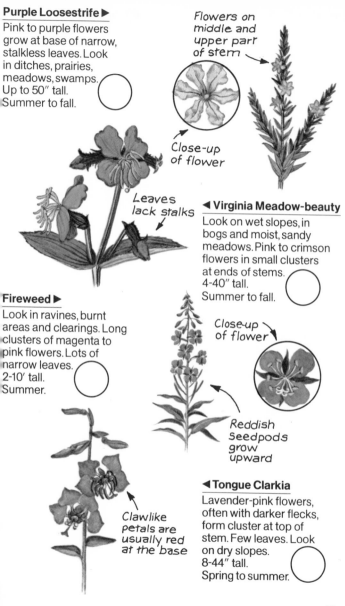

Purple Loosestrife ▶
Pink to purple flowers grow at base of narrow, stalkless leaves. Look in ditches, prairies, meadows, swamps. Up to 50" tall. Summer to fall.

Flowers on middle and upper part of stem

Close-up of flower

Leaves lack stalks

◀ Virginia Meadow-beauty
Look on wet slopes, in bogs and moist, sandy meadows. Pink to crimson flowers in small clusters at ends of stems. 4-40" tall. Summer to fall.

Fireweed ▶
Look in ravines, burnt areas and clearings. Long clusters of magenta to pink flowers. Lots of narrow leaves. 2-10' tall. Summer.

Close-up of flower

Reddish seedpods grow upward

Clawlike petals are usually red at the base

◀ Tongue Clarkia
Lavender-pink flowers, often with darker flecks, form cluster at top of stem. Few leaves. Look on dry slopes. 8-44" tall. Spring to summer.

19

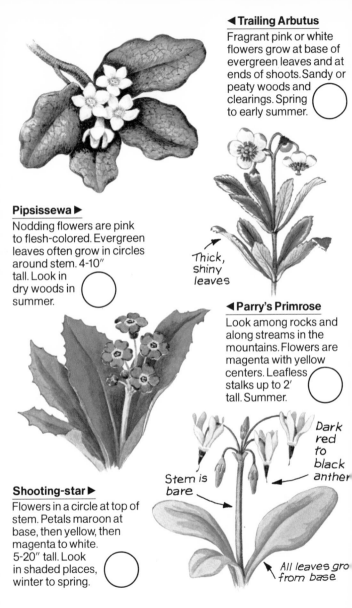

◀ Trailing Arbutus

Fragrant pink or white flowers grow at base of evergreen leaves and at ends of shoots. Sandy or peaty woods and clearings. Spring to early summer.

Pipsissewa ▶

Nodding flowers are pink to flesh-colored. Evergreen leaves often grow in circles around stem. 4-10" tall. Look in dry woods in summer.

Thick, shiny leaves

◀ Parry's Primrose

Look among rocks and along streams in the mountains. Flowers are magenta with yellow centers. Leafless stalks up to 2' tall. Summer.

Shooting-star ▶

Flowers in a circle at top of stem. Petals maroon at base, then yellow, then magenta to white. 5-20" tall. Look in shaded places, winter to spring.

Dark red to black anther

Stem is bare

All leaves grow from base

Rose-pink ▶

Fragrant flowers have pink petals, yellow centers. Leaves are stalkless. Look in clearings, open woods, prairies. 8-36" tall. Summer to fall.

Base of leaf clasps stem

Leaves borne in opposite pairs

◀ Spreading Dogbane

Plant produces a milky juice when broken. Many branches. Grows on dry soil at edges of woods and in thickets. 4-20" tall. Summer.

Gilia ▶

Stem branches form rounded flower clusters. Most leaves are at base of plant. Look in dry places in scrub. 4-12" tall. Spring.

Flowers can be violet or white

Sticky flower stalks

◀ Rose Vervain

Flowers are usually pink, rose or magenta. Look in sandy or rocky places, fields and on roadsides. Branches are 4-16" long. Spring to fall.

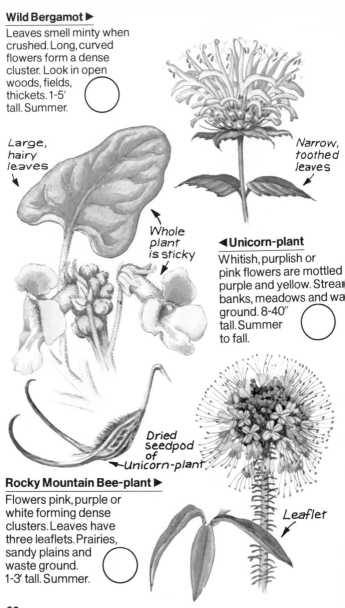

Wild Bergamot ▶

Leaves smell minty when crushed. Long, curved flowers form a dense cluster. Look in open woods, fields, thickets. 1-5' tall. Summer.

Large, hairy leaves

Narrow, toothed leaves

Whole plant is sticky

◀ Unicorn-plant

Whitish, purplish or pink flowers are mottled purple and yellow. Stream banks, meadows and waste ground. 8-40" tall. Summer to fall.

Dried seedpod of Unicorn-plant

Rocky Mountain Bee-plant ▶

Flowers pink, purple or white forming dense clusters. Leaves have three leaflets. Prairies, sandy plains and waste ground. 1-3' tall. Summer.

Leaflet

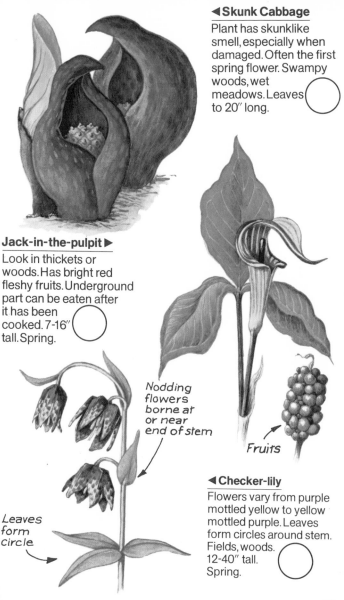

◀ Skunk Cabbage

Plant has skunklike smell, especially when damaged. Often the first spring flower. Swampy woods, wet meadows. Leaves to 20″ long.

Jack-in-the-pulpit ▶

Look in thickets or woods. Has bright red fleshy fruits. Underground part can be eaten after it has been cooked. 7-16″ tall. Spring.

Nodding flowers borne at or near end of stem

Fruits

Leaves form circle

◀ Checker-lily

Flowers vary from purple mottled yellow to yellow mottled purple. Leaves form circles around stem. Fields, woods. 12-40″ tall. Spring.

Wild Ginger ▶

A creeping plant that grows in groups. Bell shaped flower grows near ground between a pair of leaves. Moist woods, shady ledges. Spring.

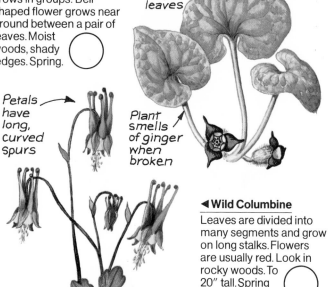

Heart or kidney shaped leaves

Petals have long, curved spurs

Plant smells of ginger when broken

◀ Wild Columbine

Leaves are divided into many segments and grow on long stalks. Flowers are usually red. Look in rocky woods. To 20″ tall. Spring to early summer.

Narrow leaves

Red Maids ▶

Flowers are rose-red to red-purple (or, rarely, white). Look in grassy places and cultivated fields. Branches 4-16″ long. Winter to spring.

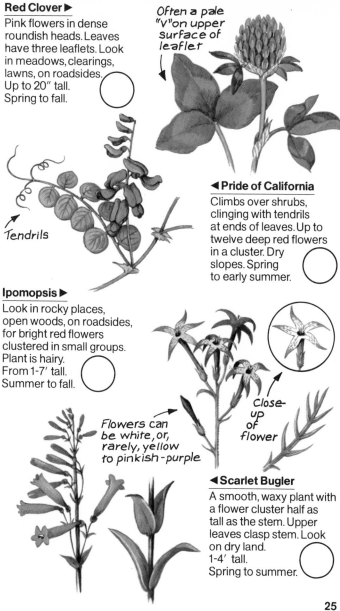

Red Clover ▶

Pink flowers in dense roundish heads. Leaves have three leaflets. Look in meadows, clearings, lawns, on roadsides. Up to 20" tall. Spring to fall.

Often a pale "V" on upper surface of leaflet

Tendrils

◀ Pride of California

Climbs over shrubs, clinging with tendrils at ends of leaves. Up to twelve deep red flowers in a cluster. Dry slopes. Spring to early summer.

Ipomopsis ▶

Look in rocky places, open woods, on roadsides, for bright red flowers clustered in small groups. Plant is hairy. From 1-7' tall. Summer to fall.

Close-up of flower

Flowers can be white, or, rarely, yellow to pinkish-purple

◀ Scarlet Bugler

A smooth, waxy plant with a flower cluster half as tall as the stem. Upper leaves clasp stem. Look on dry land. 1-4' tall. Spring to summer.

Indian Warrior ▶

Flowers borne in clusters on the end of the stem. Deeply divided leaves. Look on dry slopes, scrub, woodland, pine woods. 4-20" tall. Winter to summer.

◀ Scarlet Paintbrush

Upright plant with few stems. Narrow leaves. Look in moist, shady places in mountains. From 16-32" tall. Spring to fall.

A sticky, hairy plant

Seaside Petunia ▶

Purple or reddish-violet flowers with white or yellow tubes. Look on beaches, dried pool and stream beds. 4-16" tall. Spring to fall.

Cardinal-flower ▶

Bright red flowers. Many narrow leaves on an unbranched stem 1-6' tall. Look on damp shores, in meadows and swamps. Summer through to fall. ◯

Leaves are downy underneath ↗

Purple Blazing-star ▶

Many stems and smooth, narrow leaves. Stems bear dense clusters of purple flowers. Dry prairies and plains, late summer to fall. ◯ 6-32" tall.

Leaves are irregularly toothed ↘

◀ Ironweed

Narrow, toothed leaves and many bell-shaped heads of tubular, purple flowers. Look in moist woods in summer through to fall. ◯ 3-10' tall.

Base of flower head →

Very narrow leaves ←

◀ Bull Thistle

Main leaves and small leaves below purple flower heads are prickly. Look in pastures, clearings and on roadsides. ◯ 20-80" tall. Summer to fall.

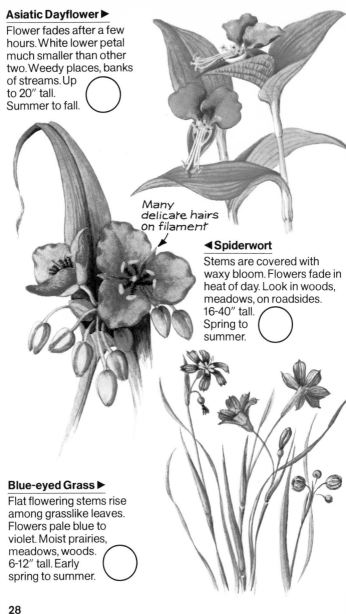

Asiatic Dayflower ▶

Flower fades after a few hours. White lower petal much smaller than other two. Weedy places, banks of streams. Up to 20″ tall. Summer to fall.

Many delicate hairs on filament

◀Spiderwort

Stems are covered with waxy bloom. Flowers fade in heat of day. Look in woods, meadows, on roadsides. 16-40″ tall. Spring to summer.

Blue-eyed Grass ▶

Flat flowering stems rise among grasslike leaves. Flowers pale blue to violet. Moist prairies, meadows, woods. 6-12″ tall. Early spring to summer.

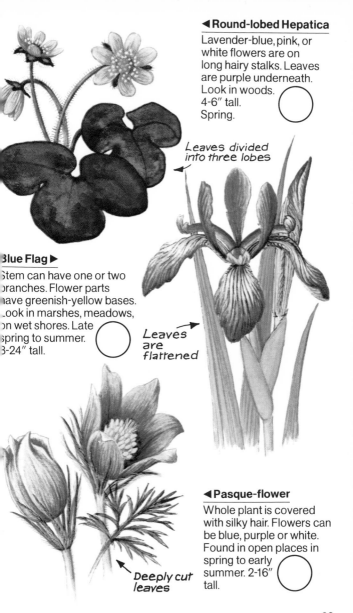

◄ Round-lobed Hepatica

Lavender-blue, pink, or white flowers are on long hairy stalks. Leaves are purple underneath. Look in woods. 4-6" tall. Spring.

Leaves divided into three lobes

Blue Flag ►

Stem can have one or two branches. Flower parts have greenish-yellow bases. Look in marshes, meadows, on wet shores. Late spring to summer. 8-24" tall.

Leaves are flattened

◄ Pasque-flower

Whole plant is covered with silky hair. Flowers can be blue, purple or white. Found in open places in spring to early summer. 2-16" tall.

Deeply cut leaves

Blue Columbine ▶
Bright blue sepals and white petals. Leaves at base are divided into roundish segments. Grows high in the mountains. 8-32" tall. Summer.

Spur (sepals forming tube)

◀ Larkspur
Flowers grow in loose clusters. Color can be blue or violet; sometimes marked with white. Look in woods and on prairies. 4-36" tall. Spring.

Leaflets attached at same point

Lupine ▶
Hairy plant with upright, slender stem. Flowers from light blue to lilac. Look in open fields and on slopes in the spring. 8-16" tall.

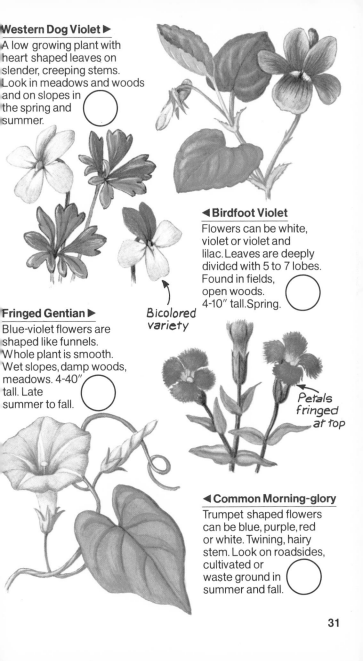

Western Dog Violet ▶

A low growing plant with heart shaped leaves on slender, creeping stems. Look in meadows and woods and on slopes in the spring and summer.

◀ Birdfoot Violet

Flowers can be white, violet or violet and lilac. Leaves are deeply divided with 5 to 7 lobes. Found in fields, open woods. 4-10" tall. Spring.

Fringed Gentian ▶

Blue-violet flowers are shaped like funnels. Whole plant is smooth. Wet slopes, damp woods, meadows. 4-40" tall. Late summer to fall.

Bicolored variety

Petals fringed at top

◀ Common Morning-glory

Trumpet shaped flowers can be blue, purple, red or white. Twining, hairy stem. Look on roadsides, cultivated or waste ground in summer and fall.

31

Wild Heliotrope ▶

Blue to purplish-blue or cream flowers. Stems can stand upright, lean or lie flat. Slopes, dunes, fields. Stems up to 50″ long. Spring to summer.

Stem is bristly

◀ Blue Phlox

Blue to purple flowers in an open rounded cluster on stems 4-20″ tall. Has few leaves. Look on rocky slopes or in woods. Spring.

Flowers can be white with black dots on petals

Baby Blue-eyes ▶

Flowers are usually bright blue with a light center. Look on slopes in grassland and scrub. Stems 4-12″ long. Winter to early summer.

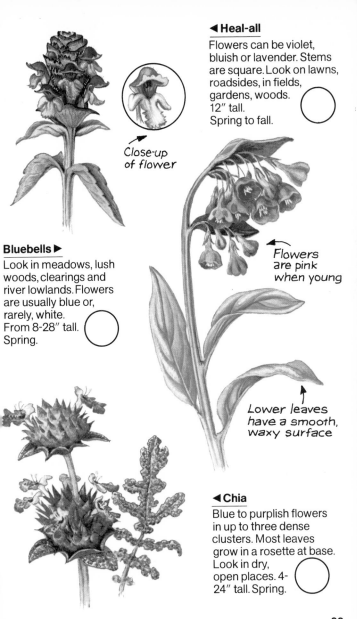

◄ Heal-all
Flowers can be violet, bluish or lavender. Stems are square. Look on lawns, roadsides, in fields, gardens, woods. 12" tall. Spring to fall.

Close-up of flower

Bluebells ►
Look in meadows, lush woods, clearings and river lowlands. Flowers are usually blue or, rarely, white. From 8-28" tall. Spring.

Flowers are pink when young

Lower leaves have a smooth, waxy surface

◄ Chia
Blue to purplish flowers in up to three dense clusters. Most leaves grow in a rosette at base. Look in dry, open places. 4-24" tall. Spring.

◄ Horse-nettle
A prickly, hairy plant. Pale violet to white star shaped flowers. Look in fields, waste ground, woods. 12-40" tall. Spring to fall.

Spines on underside of leaf

Close-up of flower

← Spur

Old-field Toadflax ►
Loose clusters of violet, spurred flowers. Narrow leaves. A very slender plant. Found in sandy places. 32" tall. Spring to fall.

Close-up of flower

◄ American Brooklime
A smooth, fleshy plant with toothed leaves. Violet or lilac flowers. Look near shallow water, swamps, streams. Up to 40" long. Summer.

Monkey-flower ►
Blue to pinkish flowers borne between upper leaves and stem. Look in meadows, near shores and other wet places. 1-4' tall. Summer to fall.

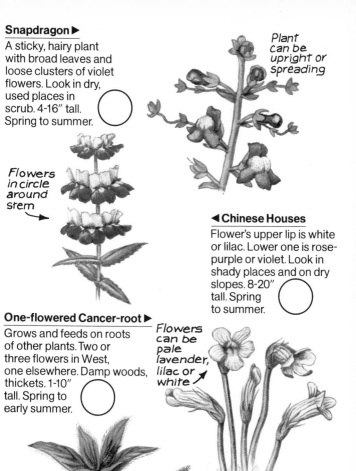

Snapdragon ▶

A sticky, hairy plant with broad leaves and loose clusters of violet flowers. Look in dry, used places in scrub. 4-16" tall. Spring to summer.

Plant can be upright or spreading

Flowers in circle around stem

◀ Chinese Houses

Flower's upper lip is white or lilac. Lower one is rose-purple or violet. Look in shady places and on dry slopes. 8-20" tall. Spring to summer.

One-flowered Cancer-root ▶

Grows and feeds on roots of other plants. Two or three flowers in West, one elsewhere. Damp woods, thickets. 1-10" tall. Spring to early summer.

Flowers can be pale lavender, lilac or white

◀ Hairy Ruellia

Almost stalkless flowers, violet to lavender, borne between upper leaves and stem. Look on prairies, in clearings, woods. 1-2' tall. Summer.

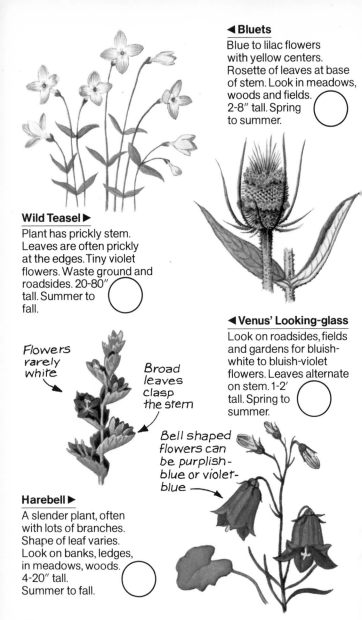

◀ Bluets

Blue to lilac flowers with yellow centers. Rosette of leaves at base of stem. Look in meadows, woods and fields. 2-8″ tall. Spring to summer.

Wild Teasel ▶

Plant has prickly stem. Leaves are often prickly at the edges. Tiny violet flowers. Waste ground and roadsides. 20-80″ tall. Summer to fall.

◀ Venus' Looking-glass

Look on roadsides, fields and gardens for bluish-white to bluish-violet flowers. Leaves alternate on stem. 1-2′ tall. Spring to summer.

Flowers rarely white

Broad leaves clasp the stem

Bell shaped flowers can be purplish-blue or violet-blue

Harebell ▶

A slender plant, often with lots of branches. Shape of leaf varies. Look on banks, ledges, in meadows, woods. 4-20″ tall. Summer to fall.

Prairie Flax ▶

Plant has very narrow leaves and leafy clusters of blue flowers. Usually has several stems. Banks, prairies, forests. 6-30" tall. Spring to fall.

◀ New England Aster

Flower heads have yellow centers and purple to pink petals. Look in fields, meadows, thickets, along roadsides. 12-40" tall. Summer to fall.

Common Chicory ▶

Flower heads are usually blue but they can be pink or white. Look on waste ground, in fields and on roadsides. 12-40" tall. Spring to fall.

Leaves lobed or toothed

Air filled base of leaf acts as a float

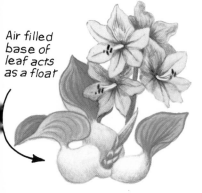

◀ Water-hyacinth

A floating plant common in ponds, streams and ditches. Showy flowers on stalks 4-16" tall. Chokes waterways in the south. Spring to summer.

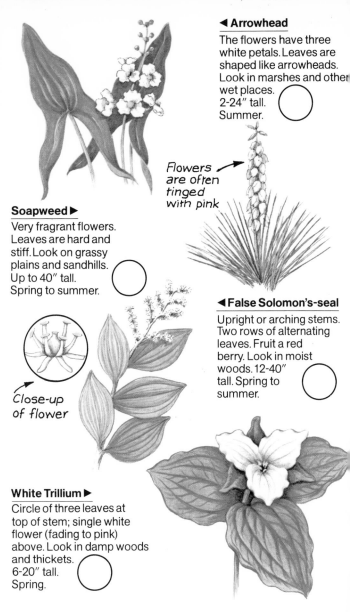

◀ Arrowhead

The flowers have three white petals. Leaves are shaped like arrowheads. Look in marshes and other wet places.
2-24″ tall.
Summer.

Flowers are often tinged with pink

Soapweed ▶

Very fragrant flowers. Leaves are hard and stiff. Look on grassy plains and sandhills.
Up to 40″ tall.
Spring to summer.

Close-up of flower

◀ False Solomon's-seal

Upright or arching stems. Two rows of alternating leaves. Fruit a red berry. Look in moist woods. 12-40″ tall. Spring to summer.

White Trillium ▶

Circle of three leaves at top of stem; single white flower (fading to pink) above. Look in damp woods and thickets.
6-20″ tall.
Spring.

38

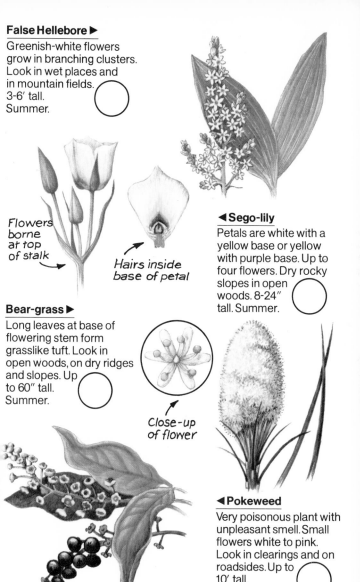

False Hellebore ▶

Greenish-white flowers grow in branching clusters. Look in wet places and in mountain fields. 3-6' tall. Summer.

Flowers borne at top of stalk

Hairs inside base of petal

◀ Sego-lily

Petals are white with a yellow base or yellow with purple base. Up to four flowers. Dry rocky slopes in open woods. 8-24" tall. Summer.

Bear-grass ▶

Long leaves at base of flowering stem form grasslike tuft. Look in open woods, on dry ridges and slopes. Up to 60" tall. Summer.

Close-up of flower

◀ Pokeweed

Very poisonous plant with unpleasant smell. Small flowers white to pink. Look in clearings and on roadsides. Up to 10' tall. Summer to fall.

◀ Miner's Lettuce

Found mainly in moist, shady places. Was eaten as a salad by American Indian miners and settlers. 12" tall. Winter, spring to summer.

Stems grow through center of leaf

Close-up of flower

Common Chickweed ▶

Look on cultivated ground, waste ground, in woods and thickets. Small white flowers. Trailing stems up to 32" long. From spring to fall.

◀ Anemone

Found in woods and on prairies. Leaves on stems have no stalks and grow in a circle around stem. One to six flowers. 8-28" tall. Spring to early summer.

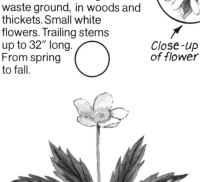

Nodding flowers

Sepals

Early Meadow-rue ▶

Plant has drooping flowers and leaves. Four or five sepals vary from greenish-white to purplish-brown. Moist woods. 8-30" tall. Spring.

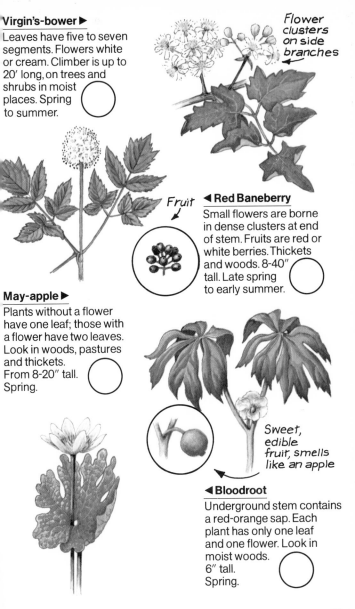

Virgin's-bower ▶

Leaves have five to seven segments. Flowers white or cream. Climber is up to 20' long, on trees and shrubs in moist places. Spring to summer.

Flower clusters on side branches

Fruit

◀ Red Baneberry

Small flowers are borne in dense clusters at end of stem. Fruits are red or white berries. Thickets and woods. 8-40" tall. Late spring to early summer.

May-apple ▶

Plants without a flower have one leaf; those with a flower have two leaves. Look in woods, pastures and thickets. From 8-20" tall. Spring.

Sweet, edible fruit, smells like an apple

◀ Bloodroot

Underground stem contains a red-orange sap. Each plant has only one leaf and one flower. Look in moist woods. 6" tall. Spring.

Prickly Poppy ▶

Has fleshy leaves. Sap is bright yellow. Look in waste ground, on prairies, hills and roadsides. 16-32″ tall. Spring to early fall.

◀ Dutchman's-breeches

Between four and ten hanging flowers, usually white with cream tips. Finely divided leaves. Look in woods. 8-12″ tall. Spring.

Leaves grow from base of plant

Grass-of-Parnassus ▶

White petals have green or yellow veins. Each stalk bears one flower. Leaves grow from base. Wet meadows and bogs. 4-24″ tall. Summer to fall.

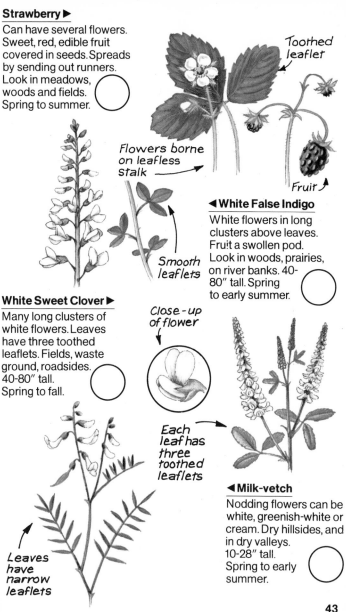

Strawberry ▶

Can have several flowers. Sweet, red, edible fruit covered in seeds. Spreads by sending out runners. Look in meadows, woods and fields. Spring to summer.

Toothed leaflet

Flowers borne on leafless stalk

Fruit

Smooth leaflets

◀ White False Indigo

White flowers in long clusters above leaves. Fruit a swollen pod. Look in woods, prairies, on river banks. 40-80" tall. Spring to early summer.

White Sweet Clover ▶

Many long clusters of white flowers. Leaves have three toothed leaflets. Fields, waste ground, roadsides. 40-80" tall. Spring to fall.

Close-up of flower

Each leaf has three toothed leaflets

◀ Milk-vetch

Nodding flowers can be white, greenish-white or cream. Dry hillsides, and in dry valleys. 10-28" tall. Spring to early summer.

Leaves have narrow leaflets

43

A circle of leaves grows where stem branches

◀ Flowering Spurge
Look in woods, prairies, fields and on roadsides. Leaves and stems contain milky juice. Flowers in rounded clusters. Up to 40" tall. Late spring to fall.

Tufted Evening-primrose ▶
Plant stemless or with a short stem. Narrow leaves. White flowers fading to pink; open near sunset. Dry, rocky slopes. 4-10" tall. Spring to fall.

◀ Wild Carrot
Clusters of flowers all white except for pink or purple one at center. Waste ground, fields and roadsides. 1-4' tall. Spring to fall.

Cow-parsnip ▶
Many tiny white flowers in big rounded clusters. Ribbed, hollow stem. Large leaves. Moist places, roadsides. 3-10' tall. Spring to summer.

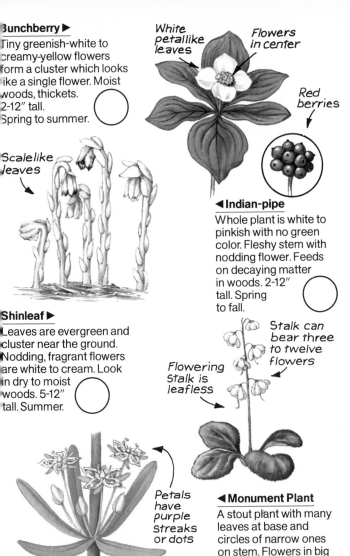

Bunchberry ▶

Tiny greenish-white to creamy-yellow flowers form a cluster which looks like a single flower. Moist woods, thickets. 2-12" tall. Spring to summer.

White petallike leaves

Flowers in center

Red berries

Scalelike leaves

◀ Indian-pipe

Whole plant is white to pinkish with no green color. Fleshy stem with nodding flower. Feeds on decaying matter in woods. 2-12" tall. Spring to fall.

Shinleaf ▶

Leaves are evergreen and cluster near the ground. Nodding, fragrant flowers are white to cream. Look in dry to moist woods. 5-12" tall. Summer.

Stalk can bear three to twelve flowers

Flowering stalk is leafless

Petals have purple streaks or dots

◀ Monument Plant

A stout plant with many leaves at base and circles of narrow ones on stem. Flowers in big clusters. Open pine woods. 3-7' tall. Summer.

45

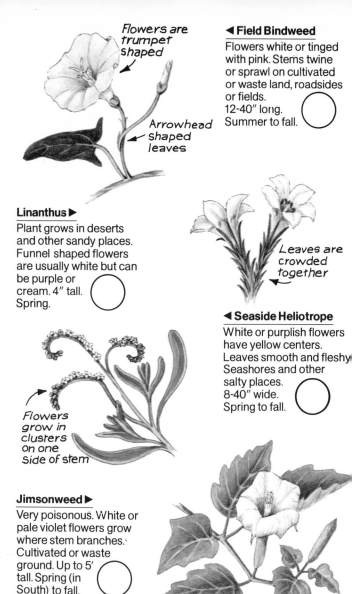

Flowers are trumpet shaped

Arrowhead shaped leaves

◄ Field Bindweed
Flowers white or tinged with pink. Stems twine or sprawl on cultivated or waste land, roadsides or fields.
12-40" long.
Summer to fall.

Linanthus ►
Plant grows in deserts and other sandy places. Funnel shaped flowers are usually white but can be purple or cream. 4" tall. Spring.

Leaves are crowded together

◄ Seaside Heliotrope
White or purplish flowers have yellow centers. Leaves smooth and fleshy. Seashores and other salty places.
8-40" wide.
Spring to fall.

Flowers grow in clusters on one side of stem

Jimsonweed ►
Very poisonous. White or pale violet flowers grow where stem branches. Cultivated or waste ground. Up to 5' tall. Spring (in South) to fall.

46

Beardtongue ▶

Flowers are white or white tinted with purple. Leaves smooth with sharp points. Look in meadows, open woods. Up to 5' tall. Spring to summer.

Flowers are bearded inside

Fruit

◀ Partridgeberry

Trailing stems form mats. Flowers borne in pairs. Evergreen leaves can have white parts. Fruit a red, edible berry. Slightly raised ground in woods. Summer.

Yerba Mansa ▶

Spikes of tiny petalless flowers with petallike leaves at base. Looks like one flower. Stream edges, wet flats, meadows. 4-20" tall. Spring to fall.

Flowers

Most leaves are at base of plant

◀ Thoroughwort

Many heads of whitish flowers in flattened clusters. Look on wet shores, in thickets and low woods. 1-5' tall. Summer to fall.

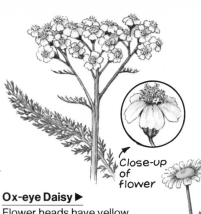

Close-up of flower

◀ Common Yarrow

Small flower heads in dense clusters. White to pinkish petals. Roadsides, fields, or in West, woods and scrub. 4-40" tall. Summer to fall. ◯

Ox-eye Daisy ▶

Flower heads have yellow centers and many white petals. Look in fields, waste ground, on roadsides. 8-40" tall. Late spring to fall. ◯

Petals can be lavender

Stem leaves are clasping

◀ Common Fleabane

Narrow, stalkless leaves. Pink to white petals with yellow centers. Banks of streams, moist thickets, shores. 4-40" tall. Spring to summer. ◯

Fragrant Water-lily ▶

Fragrant flower opens in the morning. Circular, floating leaves about 10" in diameter. Look in ponds, lakes and ditches. Summer. ◯

48

Parts of a plant

When you find a wild flower, look closely at the flower head and the leaves; this will help you to identify it. These pictures show some of the different parts of a flower, different leaf shapes and the arrangements of the leaves on the stem.

Flowers

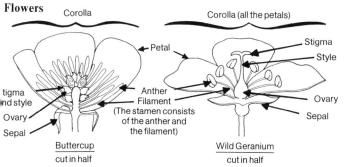

The stigma, style and ovary are the female parts of the flower, and the stamens are the male parts.

Pollen from the stamens is received by the stigma. It causes seeds to grow inside the ovary.

Leaves

There are many different leaf shapes; leaves can also be arranged in different ways on the stem.

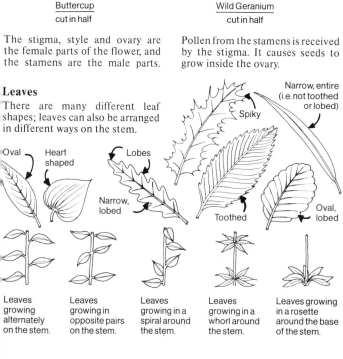

How seeds are formed

All plants produce seeds to form new plants. Pollen from the male part of the flower (the anthers) must first be received by the female part (the stigma). This process is called pollination. Pollen is the yellow powder which sticks to your fingers when you touch the center of a flower.

Pollen is usually carried from one flower to another of the same kind by insects or by wind. After pollination, the male cells from the pollen fuse (join) with the female "egg" cells in the ovary. The petals wither, the ovary swells and a fruit forms; seeds form inside the ovary.

Insect-pollinated flowers

Insects are attracted to these flowers by their bright color, scent and sometimes by a sweet liquid called nectar produced at the base of the petals. An insect lands on a flower and pollen sticks to its body; when it visits another flower of the same kind, pollen may rub off on to the stigma.

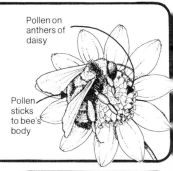

Pollen on anthers of daisy

Pollen sticks to bee's body

Wind-pollinated flowers

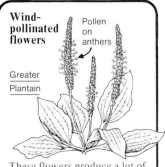

Pollen on anthers

Greater Plantain

These flowers produce a lot of light pollen which is carried by the wind to other flowers of the same kind. They do not need to attract insects, and are not brightly colored or scented and do not produce nectar.

Flower to fruit: Strawberry

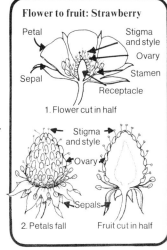

Petal
Sepal
Stigma and style
Ovary
Stamen
Receptacle

1. Flower cut in half

Stigma and style
Ovary
Sepals

2. Petals fall   Fruit cut in half

How seeds are spread

The seeds inside the fruit must now be released so that the following year they will take root and begin to grow. They must also find new places to grow in. The seeds are scattered in many different ways (see the pictures below). Look at the fruits you find on wild flowers and try to figure out how they spread their seeds.

Seeds may stay alive for months or years until the right balance of water, warmth and air makes them grow. Then a shoot will grow up from the seed and a root will grow down into the soil. The plant will then flower and the whole process will begin again.

Seeds spread by animals

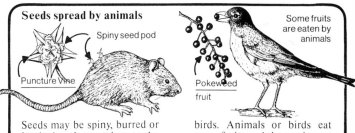

Spiny seed pod

Puncture Vine

Some fruits are eaten by animals

Pokeweed fruit

Seeds may be spiny, burred or hooked so they catch on to the coats of animals or feathers of birds. Animals or birds eat some fruits and the seeds pass through their bodies.

Seeds spread by wind

Some fruits and seeds have special features that enable them to be carried away from the parent plant in the wind.

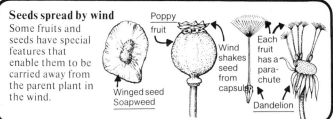

Poppy fruit

Winged seed Soapweed

Wind shakes seed from capsule

Each fruit has a parachute

Dandelion

Seeds spread by explosion

Some plants form pods which explode or twist open, scattering seeds away from plant.

Creeping Lady's-sorrel

Seeds spread by water

Some fruits and seeds can float in water and may be carried away in the water current.

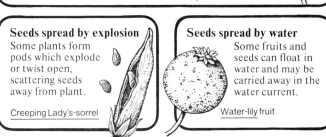

Water-lily fruit

Where to look

Here are some of the places where you could look for wild flowers, and the sort of flowers you may find in them.

Towns: You may see flowers growing in the cracks of sidewalks and walls, as well as in vacant lots, railroad yards, parking lots and gardens. Their seeds are usually spread by wind. They must be tough to live in the poor soils and dirty air.

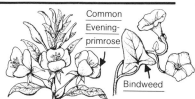

Common Evening-primrose

Bindweed

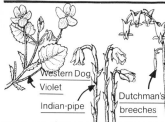

Western Dog Violet

Indian-pipe

Dutchman's breeches

Forests: The best time to look for flowers in forests is in spring, before the leaves of the trees start to grow and keep the sunlight from reaching the forest floor. Most plants need light to grow. One species which can live in the dim light of the summer forest is the Indian Pipe, which feeds on dead leaves.

Seashore: The plants you will find on the shore must survive strong winds, harsh sunlight, salt spray and lack of fresh water. Like desert plants, many have long roots to search out water deep in the sand; their long roots and fleshy leaves also help them to grip the mud, sand or stones and keep them from blowing over.

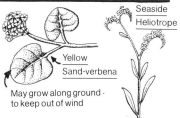

Seaside Heliotrope

Yellow Sand-verbena

May grow along ground to keep out of wind

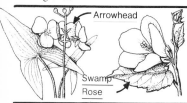

Arrowhead

Swamp Rose

Marshes and swamps: Many wetland plants have thick, tangled root systems that trap mud; this gives them a firmer base from which to grow and helps to raise them above water. But be careful when you are looking here, and stay on paths.

Fields and roadsides: Look on the edges of fields where crops are grown. The plants you will find on roadsides are hardy and can survive the exhaust fumes of cars.

Prairies and plains: Wild flowers growing here must be hardy enough to survive summer droughts and strong winds; they help protect the soil if the grasses wither.

How plants adapt

Plants grow in many places – including water, on mountains and even the desert. Here are some of the ways in which flowering plants have adapted, enabling them to grow in these places.

Deserts

The wild flowers you find in the desert show how well plants can adapt to difficult conditions.

Plants lose water through their leaves, so many desert plants have small leaves to help prevent this. Many of course shed their leaves quite regularly during dry seasons.

Notice that desert plants are often widely, and evenly, spaced; this is to give each plant a large area from which to draw water. Many plants have long roots to search out water deep in the ground.

The seeds of desert plants are very tough and able to remain alive without growing for years. As soon as the rainfall has been heavy enough, they sprout and flower. Some plants will complete their life cycle, that is flower and produce fruit, in a very short time to take advantage of more moist conditions.

Cacti are especially well adapted to life in the desert. They can store water inside their thick, fleshy stems. Their spines protect them from being eaten by thirsty animals. They have no leaves, so no water is lost in this way.

Eastern Prickly-pear

Small leaflets to help stop water loss

Water stored inside fleshy stem

Has no leaves so no water lost in this way

Linanthus

Very small leaves

Tufted Evening-primrose

Ipomopsis

Desert plants are widely spaced so that they each have a large area from which to draw water.

California Poppy

53

How plants adapt

Mountains

Although they look delicate, wild flowers growing in the mountains are some of the hardiest of plants.

Many grow in low thick mats, hugging the ground to keep out of the wind and to trap warmer air from the soil. Some have hairy stems to help trap heat. Many also contain a chemical in their fluid which stops them freezing.

Some plants will seem to flower all spring and summer: they begin to bloom on the lower slopes in the spring, and may then flower higher and higher up the mountain as summer comes and the snow melts.

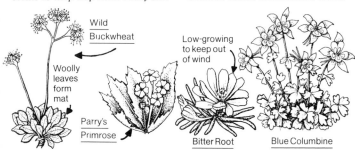

Wild Buckwheat

Woolly leaves form mat

Parry's Primrose

Low-growing to keep out of wind

Bitter Root

Blue Columbine

Rivers, Streams, Ponds and Lakes

Look on the banks and in the water itself for wild flowers. Plants growing in the water may be rooted to the bottom, like the Water-lily, or float freely, like Bladderwort.

The Water-lily leaf, or pad, is well adapted to water life; it has air sacs inside to help keep it afloat.

The top surface of the pad is waxy and water runs off it.

Only the flowering stem of the Bladderwort shows above the water. Its floating "leaves" have small sacs called bladders, which trap tiny animals in the water for food.

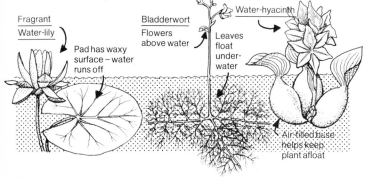

Fragrant Water-lily

Pad has waxy surface – water runs off

Bladderwort Flowers above water

Leaves float underwater

Water-hyacinth

Air-filled base helps keep plant afloat

54

Flower record book

Keep a record of all the wild flowers you find. If you use a loose-leaf binder you can add pages whenever you wish.

Take a full page for each flower you find. Draw or paint the plant, including its stem and leaves; make notes beside the picture of where and when you found the flower, its height and any other interesting points you notice.

If you are certain that a flower is a very common and widespread one, and as long as you do not find it in a park where collecting is not permitted, you can pick it and press it. Put the flower between two sheets of blotting paper and rest some heavy books on top. When the flower is dry, put a bit of glue on the stem and carefully stick it to the inside of a clear plastic bag. Then stick the bag to a page in your book with sticky tape.

But remember that many species have now become very rare because they have so often been picked.

Photographing flowers

Photographs also make a good record of the flowers you find. Here are some tips to help you to take successful photographs.

Use a color film (slides are cheaper). Always take photographs with the sun behind you and make sure that your shadow does not fall on the flower. Try to photograph the whole plant so that the stem and leaves are visible.

With a simple camera, you cannot photograph flowers in close-up. A tall plant with large flowers or a patch of creeping plants will make good photographs.

If you lie flat on the ground and photograph a flower from below, outlined against the sky, it will stand out clearly; or you can prop a piece of black or colored cardboard up behind a flower to separate it from grass and leaves in the background.

Conservation of wild flowers

There are thousands of different kinds of wild flowers in America but this great variety, like plant life in many other parts of the world, is being threatened by various human actions.

Plants have been over-picked

In many areas, especially near big cities, some kinds of flowers have so often been picked by people (for bouquets or for study) that they have become rare.

It is now against the law to pick wild flowers in all national parks and in some state parks and forests. Certain flowers are also protected by law wherever they grow: it is illegal to pick California Poppies anywhere in California; and in New York state many plants, such as Trailing Arbutus, Harebell and Lady's-slipper, are also protected by law.

You can learn more about a flower from seeing it growing in the wild than by taking it home. So never pick a flower unless you are sure that you have identified it correctly and found that it is very common and not protected by law.

Habitats are being destroyed

A wild flower will reseed itself if its habitat (the sort of place where it lives) is not disturbed. But many habitats are being disturbed and destroyed by the spread of human civilization: cities and suburbs are expanding into fields and woodlands; marshes and swamps are being drained; and even the desert is being invaded by people looking for cheap land.

Habitats are being polluted

Fumes and gases from factories and cars pollute the air, making it hard for plants to breathe; they may also harm the insects needed for pollination. Pollution of soil and water is also harmful to plants.

What you can do

- If you are walking in a park, keep on the paths. Don't trample the flowers, and don't pick them.
- If you see other people picking wild flowers, explain why they shouldn't do this – because many are endangered, and once they have all been picked it will be too late to protect them.
- Join a conservation society (see page 57).

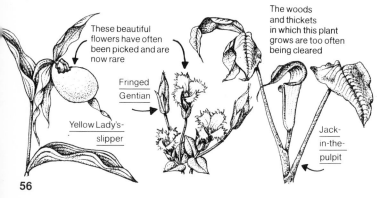

These beautiful flowers have often been picked and are now rare

Fringed Gentian

Yellow Lady's-slipper

The woods and thickets in which this plant grows are too often being cleared

Jack-in-the-pulpit

Books to read

Flowers. Herbert Zim and Alexander Martin (Golden Press). An inexpensive paperback. Color plates; flowers are arranged by color with range maps.
Newcomb's Wildflower Guide. Lawrence Newcomb (Little, Brown Co.). Covers northeast and north-central America. Flowers are arranged by key (explained). Color plates and black-and-white drawings. A good field guide.
A Field Guide to Wildflowers. Roger Tory Peterson and Margaret McKenny (Houghton, Mifflin Co.). Covers northeast and north-central North America. Flowers are arranged by color. Color plates and black-and-white drawings. A good field guide. Paperback, in the Peterson Field Guide series.
A Field Guide to Pacific States Wildflowers. Theodore F. Niehaus and Charles L. Ripper (Houghton, Mifflin Co.). Covers Washington, Oregon, California and near by areas. Hardcover, also in the Peterson Field Guide series, arranged and illustrated as above.
Wildflowers of Eastern America. John Klimas and James Cunningham (Knopf). A good identification book, has 304 color photos, but too big to put in your pocket. Flowers are arranged by color.
Wildflowers of Western America. Robert and Margaret Orr. Companion volume, same as above.
The Audubon Society Book of Wildflowers. Les Line and Walter Hodge (Abrams). A large, expensive book with nearly 200 color photos and an informative text.
Wildflowers of the United States. Harold Rickett (New York Botanical Garden). The most comprehensive book about wild-flowers in the US. There are 6 volumes, one for each major region. Flowers are arranged by family. There are color photos and black-and-white drawings. This reference work can be found in some large public libraries.

Organizations you can join

A few of the nationwide conservation organizations are listed below. Most states also have conservation organizations, as do many communities.
American Museum of Natural History, Central Park West at 79 Street, New York, NY 10024.
Friends of the Earth, 124 Spear Street, San Francisco, CA 94105.
National Wildlife Federation, 1412 16 Street NW, Washington, DC 20036.
The Nature Conservancy,
1800 N. Kent Street, Arlington, VA 22209.
New England Wildflower Society, Inc., Hemenway Road, Framingham, MA 01701.
Sierra Club, 530 Bush Street, San Francisco, CA 94108.
The Wilderness Society, 1901 Pennsylvania Avenue NW, Washington, DC 20006.
Montreal Botanical Gardens, 4101 Sherbrooke Street, Montreal.

*Have local chapters.

Scorecard

When you have seen and identified a wild flower, use this scorecard to look up the number of points you have scored.

The flowers are arranged here in alphabetical order. Before looking up your score, look at the map below to find out which area you have found the plant in. You will find that the map of North America has been divided into six different areas, each of which show separate scores.

A low score (the lowest is 5) means that the flower is common and quite easy to find; the highest score is 25, and the higher the score, the rarer or more interesting the flower.

Some flowers, like Wild Carrot, are common throughout North America and therefore have a score of 5 for each area. Others, like Wood-betony, are fairly common in some areas and rare in others.

If no score is shown, this means that the flower does not grow in that area.

When you have found your score, you can either mark it in pencil in the book, or you can keep a record of your score in a notebook, making a note of the date and place where you spot the flower. Either way you can add up your total score whenever you like – at the end of each day, week or month.

Species (Name of flower)	Scores for each area						Species (Name of flower)	Scores for each area					
	1	2	3	4	5	6		1	2	3	4	5	6
Adder's-tongue, Coast					15		Buckwheat, Wild				15	15	15
Adder's-tongue, Yellow	5	15					Bugler, Scarlet				10		
Anemone	10			20	20	10	Bunchberry	15			15	10	15
Arbutus, Trailing	15	15					Buttercup, Swamp	10					20
Arrowhead	10	10	10	10	10	10	Butterfly-weed	10	10	10	15		10
Aster, New England	15	20		20	15	10	Cancer-root, One-flowered	15	15	15	15	15	15
Baby Blue-eyes				15	15		Cardinal-flower	20	20	20	20		20
Baneberry, Red	15			15	15	15	Carrot, Wild	5	5	5	5	5	5
Beardtongue	10	10	10			15	Chia				10	15	20
Bear-grass					10	10	Chicory, Common	5	5	10	5	5	5
Bee-plant, Rocky Mountain	15		20	10	10	10	Chickweed, Common	5	5	5	5	5	5
Bergamot, Wild	10	10	15				Chinese Houses				10	10	
Bindweed, Field	5	5	5	5	5	5	Clarkia, Tongue				15	15	15
Bitter Root				20	20	20	Clover, Red	5	5	5	5	5	5
Black-eyed Susan	5	5	5	10	5	5	Clover, White Sweet	5	5	5	5	5	5
Bladderwort, Greater	20	20	20	20	25	20	Columbine, Blue				20		15
Blanket-flower	15	15	10	10		10	Columbine, Wild	15	20	15			15
Blazing-star, Purple	15	20	15	20		15	Coralroot, Spotted	25	25	25	25	25	25
Blazing-star, Yellow			15	15	15		Cranesbill, Wild	10	10				20
Bleeding-heart, Western				15			Daisy, Ox-eye	5	5	10	5	5	5
Bloodroot	10	10	20			15	Dandelion, Common	5	5	5	5	5	5
Bluets	10	10					Dayflower, Asiatic	5	5	10			15
Bluebells	15	15				25	Dogbane, Spreading	5	5	10	10	5	5
Bouncing Bet	5	5	5	10	5	5	Dutchman's-breeches	10	15			20	15
Brooklime, American	10	15	10	10	10	10	Evening Primrose, Common	5	5	10		10	10

Species (Name of flower)	Scores for each area						Species (Name of flower)	Scores for each area					
	1	2	3	4	5	6		1	2	3	4	5	6
Evening Primrose, Tufted			25	15	20	15	Ipomopsis			15	15	15	15
Fiddleneck			15	10	10	15	Ironweed	10	10	25			20
Fireweed	10	20		10	10	10	Jack-in-the-pulpit	10	10	15			20
Flag, Blue	10						Jimsonweed	5	5	5	5		5
Flax, Prairie	10		10	10	10	10	Lady's-slipper, Yellow	20	20	20	25	20	20
Fleabane, Common	10	10	10	10	10	10	Lady's-thumb	5	5	5	5	5	5
Frostweed	10	25				15	Larkspur	10		15			15
Gentian, Fringed	20	25					Lily, Checker-				20	20	25
Gilia				15		25	Lily, Common Orange Day-	5	5	10			
Ginger, Wild	10	25				25	Lily, Fragrant Water-	10	10	10	10		20
Goldenrod	10	10	10		15	10	Lily, Leopard				25	20	
Gourd, Buffalo-	15		10	10	15		Lily, Sego-				20	20	15
Grass, Blue-eyed	5	5	15			20	Lily, Wood	20	20	20	20	20	20
Grass-of-Parnassus	15					25	Linanthus				10	20	25
Gumweed				5	5	10	Loosestrife, Purple	10	10				15
Harebell	15		15	15	15	15	Lupine				10		20
Heal-all	5	5	5	5	5	5	May-apple	10	10	15			25
Heliotrope, Seaside	15	5	5	5	5	5	Meadow-beauty, Virginia	15	10	10			20
Heliotrope, Wild				5	10	15	Milkwort, Yellow	20	15				
Hellebore, False				10	10	10	Miner's Lettuce				5	5	5
Hepatica, Round-lobed	10	10					Monkey-flower	10	10	25			10
Hyacinth, Water	25	5	5	25			Monkey-flower, Common	5			5	5	10
Indian-pipe	15	15	15		15	15	Monument Plant			15	15	15	15
Indian Warrior				15	15		Morning-glory, Common	5	5	5	5	5	5
Indigo, White False	10	10	20			20	Moss, Spanish	25	10	10			

Species (Name of flower)	Scores for each area						Species (Name of flower)	Scores for each area					
	1	2	3	4	5	6		1	2	3	4	5	6
Mullein, Common	5	5	5	5	5	5	Rose-pink	15	10	15			20
Mustard, Black	5	5	10	5	5	5	Rose, Swamp-	10	15				
Nettle, Horse-	5	5	5	5	5	5	Rue, Early Meadow-	10	15				20
Onion, Nodding	10	10	20	25	15	10	Ruellia, Hairy	15	10	15			
Orchis, Smaller Purple-fringed	20	25					St Johnswort, Common	5	5	5	10	5	5
Orchis, Stream			20	20	15	20	Shinleaf	20			20	25	20
Paint-brush, Scarlet				10	10	10	Shooting-star				15	15	
Parsnip, Cow	10	10		10	10	10	Silverweed	10			15	15	10
Partridgeberry	10	10	15				Skunk Cabbage	10	20				20
Pasque-flower	20		25	20	20	15	Snapdragon				10		
Pea, Partridge-	10	5	5	15		15	Soapweed	25	25	15	20		10
Petunia, Seaside	15	10	10	15	15		Solomon's-seal, False	5	5	5	5	5	5
Phlox, Blue	10	15	20			20	Sorrel, Creeping Lady's-	5	5	10	5	5	5
Pink, Deptford	5	10			10	10	Spiderwort	5	5	10			15
Pipsissewa	10	15		10	10	15	Spring-beauty	5	10	10			
Pokeweed	10	10	10				Spurge, Flowering	10	10	10			15
Poppy, California		10		15	10	10	Strawberry	5	10	10		10	10
Poppy, Prickly			10	20		10	Sunflower, Common	5	5	5	5	5	5
Prickly Pear, Eastern	15	10	10			15	Teasel, Wild	10	15			10	10
Pride of California				20			Thistle, Bull	5	5		5	5	5
Primrose, Parry's				25		20	Thoroughwort	5	5	10			10
Puccoon, Hoary	15	15				15	Tickseed	15	10	15	10	10	15
Puncture Vine	10	5	5	5	5	5	Toadflax, Old-field	10	10	10	10	10	10
Pussy Paws				10	10	20	Touch-me-not, Spotted	10	10			15	15
Red Maids				5	5		Trillium, White	10	15				

Species (Name of flower)	Scores for each area						Species (Name of flower)	Scores for each area					
	1	2	3	4	5	6		1	2	3	4	5	6
Unicorn-plant	15	15	15	20	15	20	Violet, Downy Yellow	10	20				20
Venus' Looking-glass	10	10	10	15	10	10	Violet, Western Dog	20			15	10	15
Verbena, Yellow Sand-			10	10			Virgin's-bower	20			15	15	15
Vervain, Rose	15	10	10			15	Wallflower, Western	15	20	10	5	5	5
Vetch, Hairy	5	5	10	10	5	5	Wood-betony	10	10	10	15		25
Vetch, Milk-				15	15	20	Yarrow, Common	5	5	5	5	5	5
Violet, Birdfoot	10	10	15			15	Yerba Mansa			15	10	15	20

Alternative common names

Here is a list of some other common names which are also often used; they are shown in parentheses after the name used in the field guide section.

Adder's-tongue, Coast
  (Coast Fawn Lily)
Adder's-tongue, Yellow
  (Trout-lily)
Anemone
  (Canada Anemone)
Arrowhead
  (Duck Potato)
Bear-grass
  (Elk Grass)
Blanket-flower
  (Firewheel)
Blazing-star, Purple
  (Dotted Blazing-star)
Bluebells
  (Virginia Cowslip)
Bluets
  (Quaker's Ladies)
Bunchberry
  (Dwarf Cornel)
Carrot, Wild
  (Queen Anne's Lace)
Clover, White Sweet
  (Melilot)
Cranesbill, Wild
  (Wild Geranium)
Gourd, Buffalo-
  (Stinking Gourd)
Heal-all
  (Self-heal)
Hellebore, False
  (Corn Lily)
Ipomopsis
  (Scarlet Gilia)
Pokeweed
  (Poke)
Rose, Swamp-
  (Swamp Rose-mallow)
Tickseed
  (Lance-leaved Coreopsis)
Touch-me-not, Spotted
  (Jewelweed)
Vetch, Milk-
  (Thread-leaved Locoweed)
Wood-betony
  (Lousewort)

Latin names of flowers

The common name of a flower may vary from one area of North America to another and this can often be very confusing. If you look up a flower in other books, you may find that it helps to know the flower's name in Latin as well. This list gives the Latin names of the flowers in this book, in the order in which they appear. The first name given for each page refers to the flower at the top of that page, and so on, reading down the page.

Introduction to Part 2

This section of the book will help you to identify over 80 different trees. Not all the trees shown will be common in your area, but you may see them in large parks and gardens. There is a list of places to visit on page 120.

Remember that the shape of the whole tree may vary; for example, the Tulip Tree may have a very much longer trunk than it has in the illustration on page 105; and the shape of the Blue Gum shown on page 94 may vary according to whether it has one or more than one trunk.

The shape of a tree will also vary according to its age, but you may be able to identify a young tree by its leaves and bark.

Identifying trees

This section of the book is arranged with conifers first (page 70), followed by palm trees (page 83), followed by broadleaved trees (page 85). Trees that are closely related, for example all the oaks, are grouped together.

The illustrations show important features that will help you to identify a tree at any time of the year. For most of the trees, the leaf, the bark, the shape of a tree in full leaf and its shape in winter (if the tree is deciduous) are shown. Flowers and fruits (including cones) are also sometimes illustrated if they will help you to identify the tree.

The description next to each illustration gives you additional information to help you identify trees.

Remember that there are many clues to help you to recognize a tree, so look carefully at the bark, the tree's shape and other features.

If the tree you want to identify has no leaves on it in winter, you may be able to find out what it is by examining its winter buds and shoots. A few of these are shown on page 115, and some of the descriptions in the field guide contain notes about them.

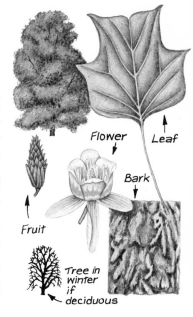

Flower   Leaf

Bark

Fruit

Tree in winter if deciduous

Beside the description is a small blank circle. Each time you spot a new tree, check it off in the circle.

Where each tree grows
At the end of the description of each tree there is a key showing the areas of North America in which the tree grows. The key refers to the following areas:

NE: Northeast   **NW: Northwest**
SE: Southeast   **SW: Southwest**
C: Central

Look at the map on page 121 to find out which area you are in.

Scorecard
There is a scorecard on pages 121-6. which gives you a separate score for each tree shown in the book, according to the area in which you see the tree. There is a separate page of scores for each of the areas.

You can also use the scorecard to find out how common a tree is in your area: a common tree scores 5 and a very rare one scores 25.

Parts of a tree

A tree is a plant that grows on a single, central woody stem. A shrub is usually smaller and has many stems.

Trees are divided into two main groups: **conifers** and **broadleaved trees.** Most broadleaved trees have broad flat leaves (which they drop in winter) and they have seeds which are enclosed in fruits (nuts or other forms). Most conifers have narrow, needlelike or scaly leaves. Their fruits are usually woody cones.

Most broadleaved trees are **deciduous** which means that they lose their leaves in the fall and grow new ones again in the spring. Most conifers are **evergreen,** meaning that they keep their green leaves throughout the winter.

These pictures show the different parts of a tree and explain some of the words that appear in this section.

Leaves

There are many different shapes of leaves. Some of the most common ones are shown here.

A leaf that is in one piece is called **simple.**

A leaf that is made up of many **leaflets** is called **compound.**

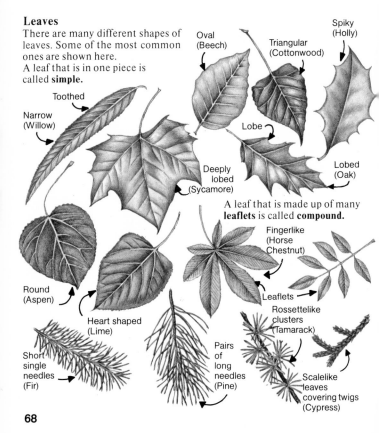

Oval (Beech)

Triangular (Cottonwood)

Spiky (Holly)

Toothed

Narrow (Willow)

Lobe

Deeply lobed (Sycamore)

Lobed (Oak)

Fingerlike (Horse Chestnut)

Round (Aspen)

Leaflets

Rossettelike clusters (Tamarack)

Heart shaped (Lime)

Short single needles (Fir)

Pairs of long needles (Pine)

Scalelike leaves covering twigs (Cypress)

68

Flowers

All trees have flowers that develop into fruits. Here are some different types of flowers.

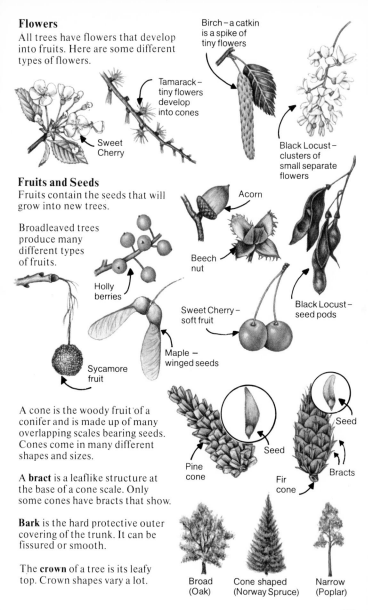

Birch – a catkin is a spike of tiny flowers

Tamarack – tiny flowers develop into cones

Sweet Cherry

Black Locust – clusters of small separate flowers

Fruits and Seeds

Fruits contain the seeds that will grow into new trees.

Broadleaved trees produce many different types of fruits.

Acorn

Beech nut

Black Locust – seed pods

Holly berries

Sweet Cherry – soft fruit

Maple – winged seeds

Sycamore fruit

A cone is the woody fruit of a conifer and is made up of many overlapping scales bearing seeds. Cones come in many different shapes and sizes.

A **bract** is a leaflike structure at the base of a cone scale. Only some cones have bracts that show.

Bark is the hard protective outer covering of the trunk. It can be fissured or smooth.

The **crown** of a tree is its leafy top. Crown shapes vary a lot.

Pine cone

Seed

Fir cone

Seed

Bracts

Broad (Oak)

Cone shaped (Norway Spruce)

Narrow (Poplar)

Shape of crown can vary

Cleft

Ginkgo is neither a conifer nor a broad-leaved tree. It is in a group on its own.

Ginkgo ▲
Leathery leaves are bright green in spring, gold in the fall. Cone shaped, brown buds. Commonly grown as a city street tree. All areas.

Corky, fissured bark

Foliage not dense

Leaves and shoots are shed in the fall

Swamp Cypress ▲
Tiny, slender leaves turn russet-brown late in the fall. Arching branches. Common along tidal creeks and near river bottoms. NE, SE & C.

Reddish-brown, spiralled bark, often peeling

Trunk swells toward base

Leaves and shoots grow in opposite pairs

Long stalked cones

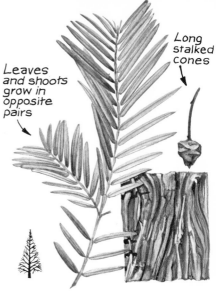

Dawn Redwood ▲

Soft, light green leaves turn red-brown and are shed in the fall. Bark has stringy orange-brown strips. Big gardens, parks. NE, SE & NW.

Shapely, slender crown

Whorls of soft, bright green leaves

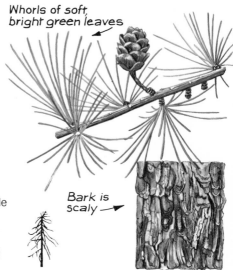

Tamarack ▲

Leaves turn yellow in the fall. Small red female flowers appear before leaves, turn purple and then turn into woody cones. NE & C.

Bark is scaly →

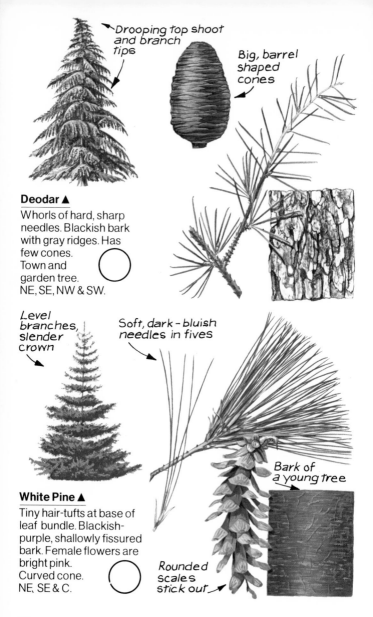

Drooping top shoot and branch tips

Big, barrel shaped cones

Deodar ▲
Whorls of hard, sharp needles. Blackish bark with gray ridges. Has few cones.
Town and garden tree.
NE, SE, NW & SW.

Level branches, slender crown

Soft, dark-bluish needles in fives

Bark of a young tree

White Pine ▲
Tiny hair-tufts at base of leaf bundle. Blackish-purple, shallowly fissured bark. Female flowers are bright pink.
Curved cone.
NE, SE & C.

Rounded scales stick out

72

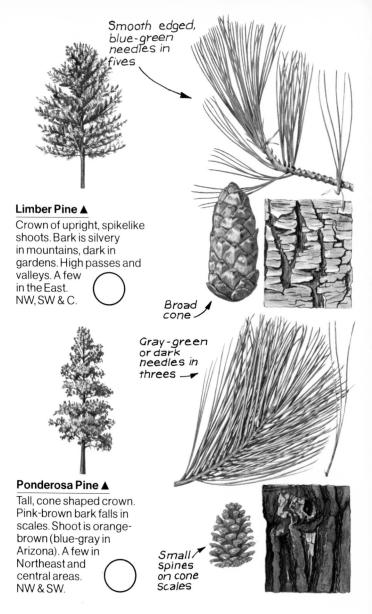

Smooth edged, blue-green needles in fives

Limber Pine ▲

Crown of upright, spikelike shoots. Bark is silvery in mountains, dark in gardens. High passes and valleys. A few in the East. NW, SW & C.

Broad cone

Gray-green or dark needles in threes →

Ponderosa Pine ▲

Tall, cone shaped crown. Pink-brown bark falls in scales. Shoot is orange-brown (blue-gray in Arizona). A few in Northeast and central areas. NW & SW.

Small spines on cone scales

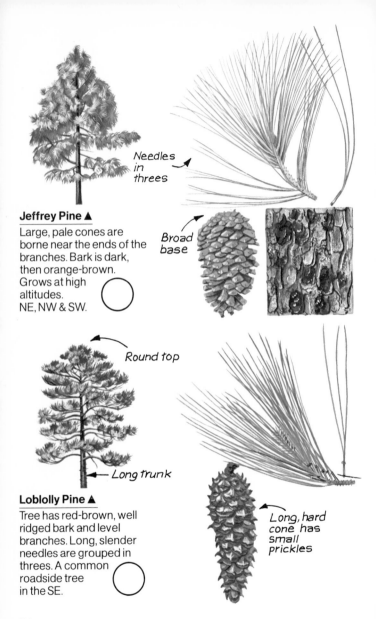

Jeffrey Pine ▲
Large, pale cones are
borne near the ends of the
branches. Bark is dark,
then orange-brown.
Grows at high
altitudes.
NE, NW & SW.

Needles in threes

Broad base

Round top

Long trunk

Loblolly Pine ▲
Tree has red-brown, well
ridged bark and level
branches. Long, slender
needles are grouped in
threes. A common
roadside tree
in the SE.

Long, hard cone has small prickles

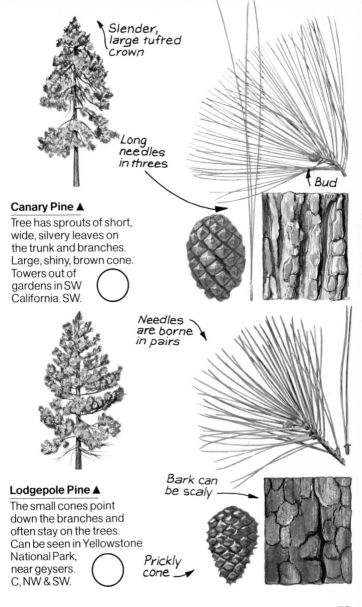

Slender, large tufted crown

Long needles in threes

Bud

Canary Pine ▲
Tree has sprouts of short, wide, silvery leaves on the trunk and branches. Large, shiny, brown cone. Towers out of gardens in SW California. SW.

Needles are borne in pairs

Lodgepole Pine ▲
The small cones point down the branches and often stay on the trees. Can be seen in Yellowstone National Park, near geysers. C, NW & SW.

Bark can be scaly

Prickly cone

75

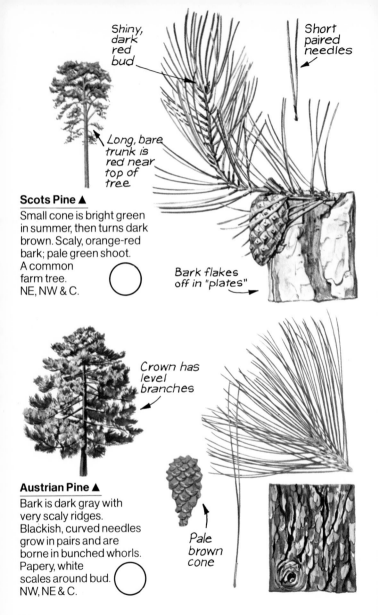

Shiny, dark red bud

Short paired needles

Long, bare trunk is red near top of tree

Scots Pine ▲
Small cone is bright green in summer, then turns dark brown. Scaly, orange-red bark; pale green shoot. A common farm tree. NE, NW & C.

Bark flakes off in "plates"

Crown has level branches

Austrian Pine ▲
Bark is dark gray with very scaly ridges. Blackish, curved needles grow in pairs and are borne in bunched whorls. Papery, white scales around bud. NW, NE & C.

Pale brown cone

Paired needles

Young shoot

Aleppo Pine ▲

Broad, light and rather fuzzy crown. Dark orange and gray bark. Common in gardens in Arizona and California. Small round buds. SW.

Shiny, reddish cones stay on tree for years

Single-leaf Nut Pine ▲

A low, bushy tree. Large flat cone has few scales, which open widely. Grows in rocky, arid areas; sometimes planted in borders. SW.

Rounded, stout, sharp needle

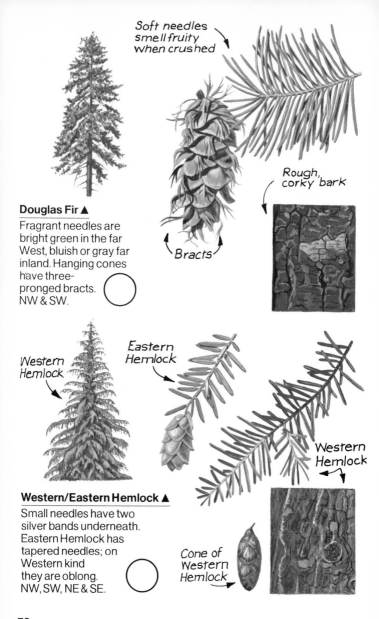

Soft needles smell fruity when crushed

Bracts

Rough, corky bark

Douglas Fir ▲

Fragrant needles are bright green in the far West, bluish or gray far inland. Hanging cones have three-pronged bracts. NW & SW.

Western Hemlock

Eastern Hemlock

Western Hemlock

Western/Eastern Hemlock ▲

Small needles have two silver bands underneath. Eastern Hemlock has tapered needles; on Western kind they are oblong. NW, SW, NE & SE.

Cone of Western Hemlock

78

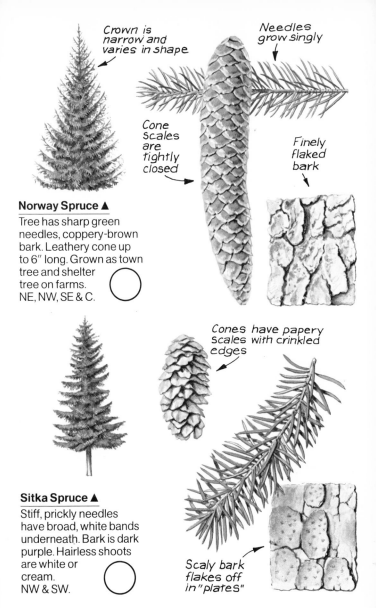

Crown is narrow and varies in shape

Needles grow singly

Cone scales are tightly closed

Finely flaked bark

Norway Spruce ▲

Tree has sharp green needles, coppery-brown bark. Leathery cone up to 6" long. Grown as town tree and shelter tree on farms. NE, NW, SE & C.

Cones have papery scales with crinkled edges

Sitka Spruce ▲

Stiff, prickly needles have broad, white bands underneath. Bark is dark purple. Hairless shoots are white or cream. NW & SW.

Scaly bark flakes off in "plates"

Blue Colorado Spruce ▲
Blue-gray, stiff needles are
curved and sharp. Very
flaky bark. Wild forms in
Wyoming are very slender.
Common
in towns.
All areas.

Buds

Cone has
whitish,
crinkled
scales

Flaky
bark

Slender
crown

Engelmann Spruce ▲
Shoot is pinkish-brown
with a few hairs. Dark
blue-green, soft needles.
Orange-brown bark.
Common in the
Rocky Mountains.
NW & C.

Scaly
bark

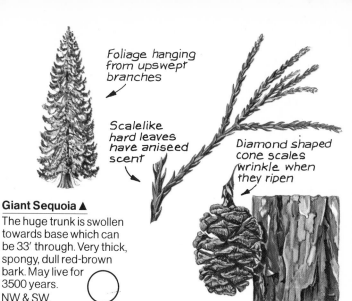

Foliage hanging from upswept branches

Scalelike hard leaves have aniseed scent

Diamond shaped cone scales wrinkle when they ripen

Giant Sequoia ▲

The huge trunk is swollen towards base which can be 33′ through. Very thick, spongy, dull red-brown bark. May live for 3500 years. NW & SW.

Needles parted on either side of shoot

Coast Redwood ▲

Hard needles have white bands underneath. Gray and orange-red bark. Small, crinkled cone. One of the world's tallest trees. NW & SW.

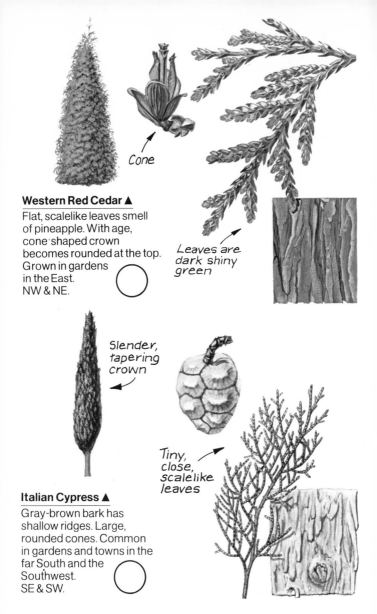

Western Red Cedar ▲

Flat, scalelike leaves smell
of pineapple. With age,
cone-shaped crown
becomes rounded at the top.
Grown in gardens
in the East.
NW & NE.

Cone

Leaves are
dark shiny
green

Slender,
tapering
crown

Tiny,
close,
scalelike
leaves

Italian Cypress ▲

Gray-brown bark has
shallow ridges. Large,
rounded cones. Common
in gardens and towns in the
far South and the
Southwest.
SE & SW.

Buds

Shapely cone shaped crown

Upright cones break up on tree in the fall

Balsam Fir ▲

Leathery, strap shaped leaves are borne on each side of the shoot. Dark, deeply fissured bark. Tree smells of balsam when handled. NE.

Fruit

Canary Palm ▲

A very sturdy palm with a huge crown. Bright green, featherlike leaves curve downward. Tree bears large bunches of pale orange flowers. SE & SW.

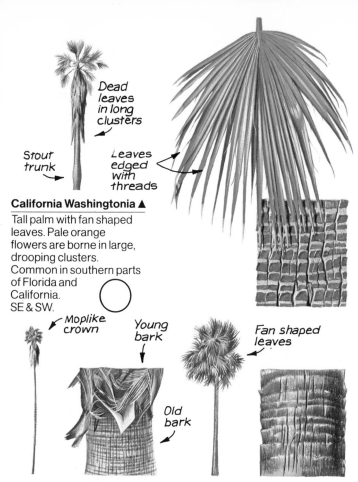

Dead leaves in long clusters

Stout trunk

Leaves edged with threads

California Washingtonia ▲

Tall palm with fan shaped leaves. Pale orange flowers are borne in large, drooping clusters. Common in southern parts of Florida and California. SE & SW.

Moplike crown

Young bark

Old bark

Fan shaped leaves

Mexican or Slender
Washingtonia ▲

Slender, slightly wavy trunk. Narrow lobed leaves are borne high up. Common in southern Florida. SW & SE.

▲ Cabbage Palmetto

Large, grayish, fan shaped leaves. Bases of leaf-stalks interlace on the trunk; stay after leaves have fallen. Rare in the Southwest. SE.

84

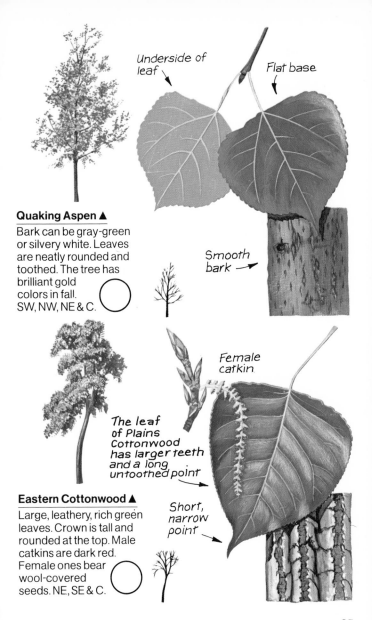

Underside of leaf

Flat base

Quaking Aspen ▲
Bark can be gray-green or silvery white. Leaves are neatly rounded and toothed. The tree has brilliant gold colors in fall. SW, NW, NE & C.

Smooth bark

Female catkin

The leaf of Plains Cottonwood has larger teeth and a long untoothed point

Eastern Cottonwood ▲
Large, leathery, rich green leaves. Crown is tall and rounded at the top. Male catkins are dark red. Female ones bear wool-covered seeds. NE, SE & C.

Short, narrow point

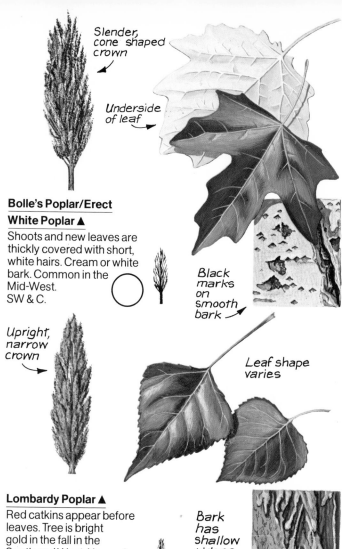

Slender, cone shaped crown

Underside of leaf

Bolle's Poplar/Erect
White Poplar ▲

Shoots and new leaves are thickly covered with short, white hairs. Cream or white bark. Common in the Mid-West.
SW & C.

Black marks on smooth bark →

Upright, narrow crown →

Leaf shape varies

Lombardy Poplar ▲

Red catkins appear before leaves. Tree is bright gold in the fall in the South and West. Narrowly pointed, small leaves. Common. All areas.

Bark has shallow ridges →

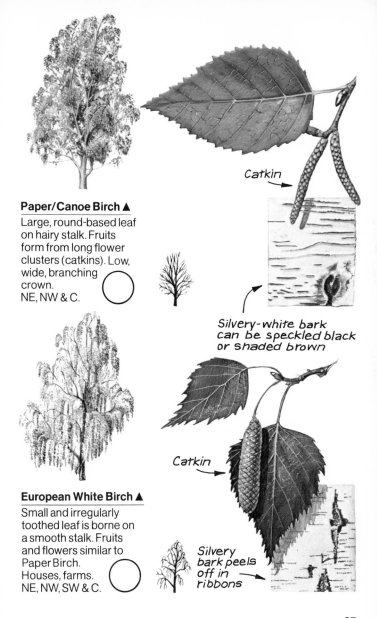

Paper/Canoe Birch ▲

Large, round-based leaf on hairy stalk. Fruits form from long flower clusters (catkins). Low, wide, branching crown.
NE, NW & C.

Catkin

Silvery-white bark can be speckled black or shaded brown

European White Birch ▲

Small and irregularly toothed leaf is borne on a smooth stalk. Fruits and flowers similar to Paper Birch.
Houses, farms.
NE, NW, SW & C.

Catkin

Silvery bark peels off in ribbons

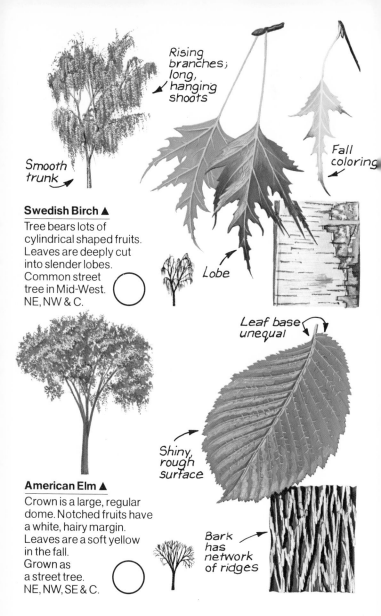

Rising branches; long, hanging shoots

Smooth trunk →

Fall coloring ←

Swedish Birch ▲
Tree bears lots of cylindrical shaped fruits. Leaves are deeply cut into slender lobes. Common street tree in Mid-West. NE, NW & C.

Lobe

Leaf base unequal

Shiny, rough surface

American Elm ▲
Crown is a large, regular dome. Notched fruits have a white, hairy margin. Leaves are a soft yellow in the fall. Grown as a street tree. NE, NW, SE & C.

Bark has network of ridges →

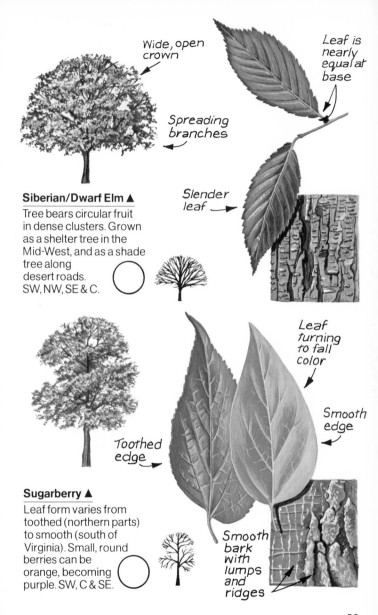

Wide, open crown

Leaf is nearly equal at base

Spreading branches

Slender leaf

Siberian/Dwarf Elm ▲
Tree bears circular fruit in dense clusters. Grown as a shelter tree in the Mid-West, and as a shade tree along desert roads. SW, NW, SE & C.

Leaf turning to fall color

Smooth edge

Toothed edge

Sugarberry ▲
Leaf form varies from toothed (northern parts) to smooth (south of Virginia). Small, round berries can be orange, becoming purple. SW, C & SE.

Smooth bark with lumps and ridges

89

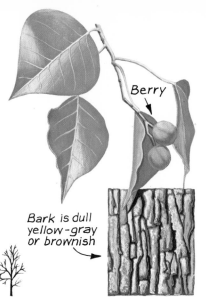

Berry

Chinese Tallow Tree ▲

Yellow flowers grow in a long spike. Fruit is a shiny, flattened berry. Leaves are on smooth, long, slender stalks. Shoots are light green.
SE & SW.

Bark is dull yellow-gray or brownish

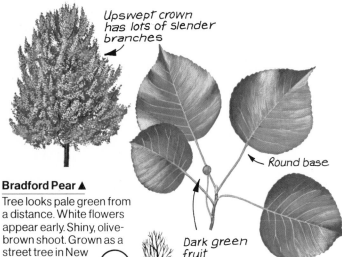

Upswept crown has lots of slender branches

Round base

Bradford Pear ▲

Tree looks pale green from a distance. White flowers appear early. Shiny, olive-brown shoot. Grown as a street tree in New York and other cities. SE & C.

Dark green fruit speckled buff

90

Upper branches grow upward

Leaves turn red in fall

Sweet Cherry/Gean ▲

Tree has lots of single white flowers in the spring. Leaves on dark red stalk. Common in British Columbia, New England. NW & NE.

Cherry (not edible)

Horizontal strips on shiny bark

Thick, cone shaped crown

American Linden ▲

Gray-brown bark is deeply fissured. Sharply toothed leaves are rich green on both sides. Shoot and bud are green. Common street tree. NE, SE, NW & C.

Leaf uneven at base

Fruit

Rounded at the top

Underside of leaf is pale and hairy

Fruits

Small-leafed European Linden ▲

Small, pale yellow flowers are very fragrant. Shoots are red-brown; buds are dark red. Common street tree in northern USA, southern Canada.
NE, SE, NW & C.

Open, widely branched crown

Leaf is hairy beneath

Empress Tree ▲

Bark is gray-brown and smooth. Lilac-blue, trumpet shaped flowers. Very big, floppy leaf is broader in young trees.
NE, SE, NW & SW.

Sticky fruit

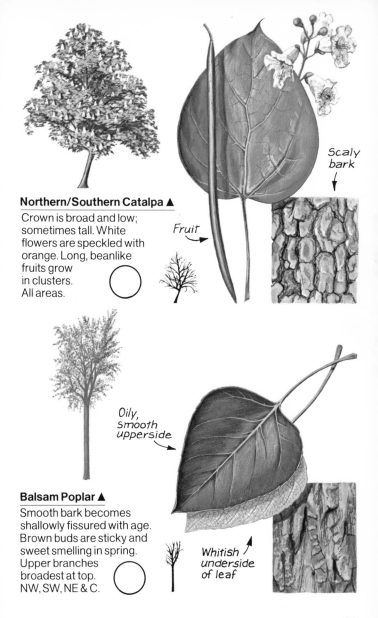

Northern/Southern Catalpa ▲

Crown is broad and low;
sometimes tall. White
flowers are speckled with
orange. Long, beanlike
fruits grow
in clusters.
All areas.

Scaly bark

Fruit

Balsam Poplar ▲

Smooth bark becomes
shallowly fissured with age.
Brown buds are sticky and
sweet smelling in spring.
Upper branches
broadest at top.
NW, SW, NE & C.

Oily, smooth upperside

Whitish underside of leaf

93

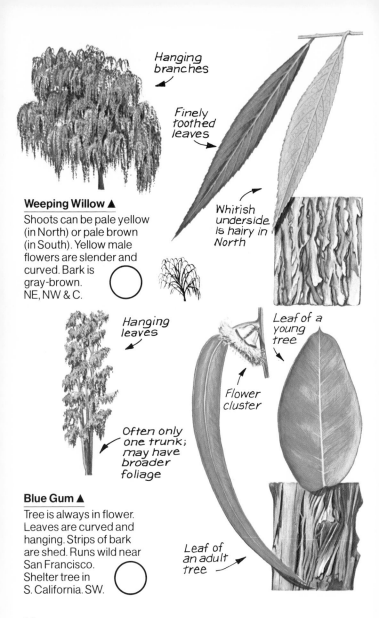

Hanging branches

Finely toothed leaves

Whitish underside is hairy in North

Weeping Willow ▲

Shoots can be pale yellow (in North) or pale brown (in South). Yellow male flowers are slender and curved. Bark is gray-brown. NE, NW & C.

Hanging leaves

Leaf of a young tree

Flower cluster

Often only one trunk; may have broader foliage

Blue Gum ▲

Tree is always in flower. Leaves are curved and hanging. Strips of bark are shed. Runs wild near San Francisco. Shelter tree in S. California. SW.

Leaf of an adult tree

Red Gum ▲

Very small fruit has a beak at the tip. Flowers are white. Commonly grown for shelter from Southern Arizona to San Diego. SW.

Russian Olive ▲

Underside of leaf is pale gray and hairy. Yellow berries borne on hanging shoots. Shoot is covered in soft, white, dense hairs. SW & C.

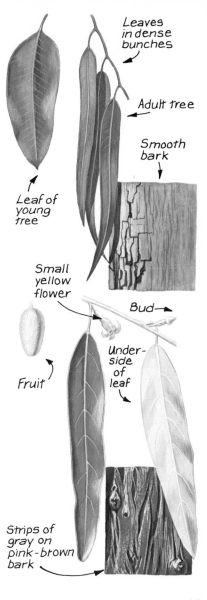

Leaves in dense bunches

Adult tree

Smooth bark

Leaf of young tree

Small yellow flower

Bud →

Fruit

Under-side of leaf

Strips of gray on pink-brown bark

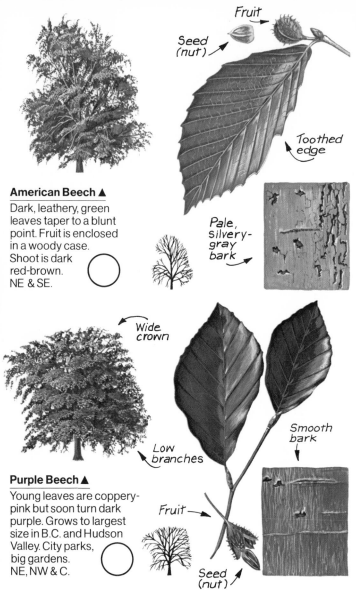

Fruit

Seed (nut)

Toothed edge

American Beech ▲
Dark, leathery, green leaves taper to a blunt point. Fruit is enclosed in a woody case. Shoot is dark red-brown.
NE & SE.

Pale, silvery-gray bark

Wide crown

Low branches

Smooth bark

Purple Beech ▲
Young leaves are coppery-pink but soon turn dark purple. Grows to largest size in B.C. and Hudson Valley. City parks, big gardens.
NE, NW & C.

Fruit →

Seed (nut)

Blackjack Oak ▲

Rough bark has dark
blackish-gray ridges.
Crown is broad and low.
Broad leaf widens into
huge lobes at tip.
Common in
roadside thickets.
SE & C.

Spiny teeth

Fall color
of leaves

Red Oak ▲

Acorns are very small in
the first year, swell in the
second year. Dark gray
bark has flat ridges
between black
fissures.
NE, NW, SE & C.

Acorn

Fall color is orange or red

White Oak ▲

A broad tree with straight branches. Slightly shaggy, pale gray bark has black fissures. Leaves have very deep, curved lobes. C, SE & NE.

Acorn

Post Oak ▲

Brownish-gray bark is closely fissured. Leaves are pale yellowish-gray on the underside. Shoot is covered in soft, orange-brown hairs. NE, SE & C.

Acorn

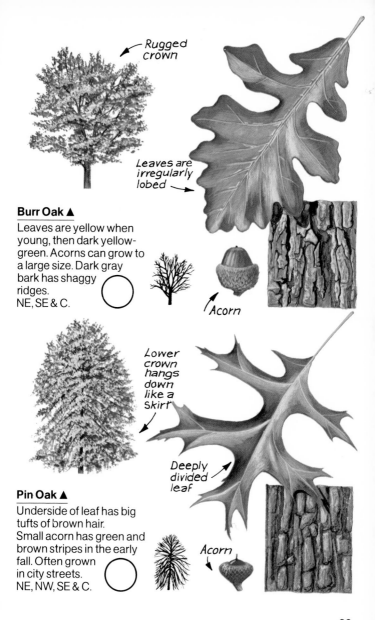

Burr Oak ▲
Leaves are yellow when young, then dark yellow-green. Acorns can grow to a large size. Dark gray bark has shaggy ridges.
NE, SE & C.

Rugged crown

Leaves are irregularly lobed →

Acorn

Pin Oak ▲
Underside of leaf has big tufts of brown hair. Small acorn has green and brown stripes in the early fall. Often grown in city streets.
NE, NW, SE & C.

Lower crown hangs down like a skirt

Deeply divided leaf

Acorn

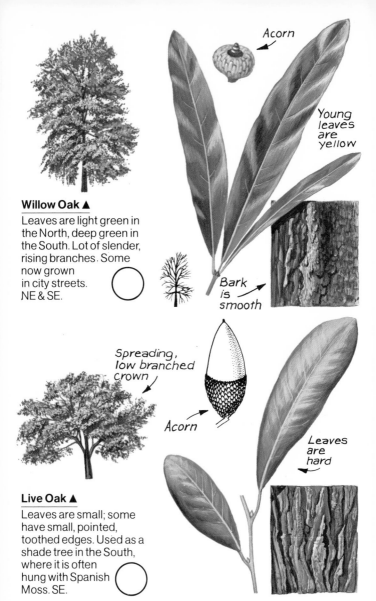

Willow Oak ▲
Leaves are light green in the North, deep green in the South. Lot of slender, rising branches. Some now grown in city streets. NE & SE.

Acorn

Young leaves are yellow

Bark is smooth

Spreading, low branched crown

Acorn

Leaves are hard

Live Oak ▲
Leaves are small; some have small, pointed, toothed edges. Used as a shade tree in the South, where it is often hung with Spanish Moss. SE.

Upright branches at top

Prickly fruit

Sharp teeth

Sweet Gum ▲

Leaves have a sweet fragrance when crushed. Bright green leaves turn brilliant red and crimson in the fall.
Long, slender top.
All areas.

Rough, ridged bark

Big, spreading crown

Toothed lobes

Buttonwood/Sycamore ▲

Leaf can be very broad and toothed, or narrower with few teeth. Bark flakes to show cream or bluish-white. New leaves yellow-gray.
SE, NE & C.

Fruit single or in groups of 3 to 5

101

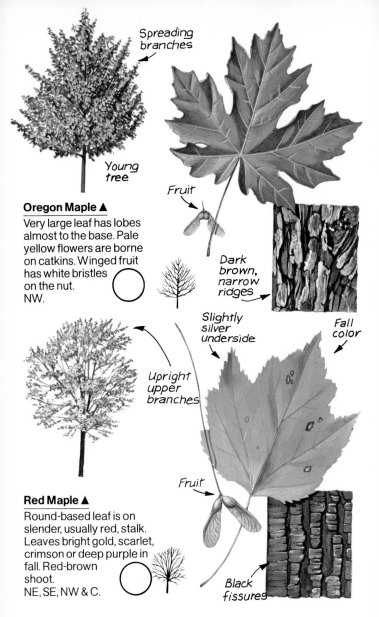

Spreading branches

Young tree

Oregon Maple ▲

Very large leaf has lobes almost to the base. Pale yellow flowers are borne on catkins. Winged fruit has white bristles on the nut. NW.

Fruit

Dark brown, narrow ridges

Slightly silver underside

Fall color

Upright upper branches

Red Maple ▲

Round-based leaf is on slender, usually red, stalk. Leaves bright gold, scarlet, crimson or deep purple in fall. Red-brown shoot. NE, SE, NW & C.

Fruit

Black fissures

Silver Maple ▲
Unusual crown has long,
upright branches at top.
Sprouts appear on the
tree trunk. Scaly, shaggy
bark is dark
gray.
All areas.

*Under-
side of
leaf is
silvery*

*Winged
fruit*

*Lobes
have
blunt
teeth*

*Winged
fruit*

Sugar Maple ▲
Leaves are very bright
orange to scarlet in the
fall. Shoots are green and
smooth. Commonly grown
along town
roadsides in NE.
NW, NE, SE & C.

*Shaggy
bark*

103

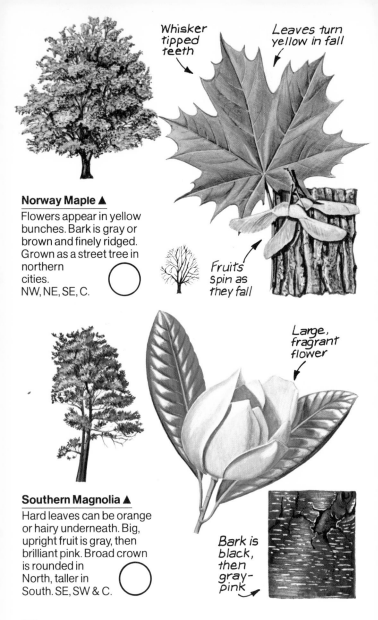

Whisker tipped teeth

Leaves turn yellow in fall

Norway Maple ▲

Flowers appear in yellow bunches. Bark is gray or brown and finely ridged. Grown as a street tree in northern cities.
NW, NE, SE, C.

Fruits spin as they fall

Large, fragrant flower

Southern Magnolia ▲

Hard leaves can be orange or hairy underneath. Big, upright fruit is gray, then brilliant pink. Broad crown is rounded in North, taller in South. SE, SW & C.

Bark is black, then gray-pink

Cone like
fruit

Ridged
bark

Trunk
sometimes
very much longer

Tulip Tree ▲
Old trees have big
branches borne high on a
clear trunk. Upright fruit
stays on tree in winter.
Greenish-yellow
flower.
NE, SE, NW & SW.

Long outer
Shoots arch
down

White fruit
turns pink
and red

White Mulberry ▲
Leaves on flowering
branches are small,
oval, and shiny dark
green. Bark is gray
with shallow
brown fissures.
All areas.

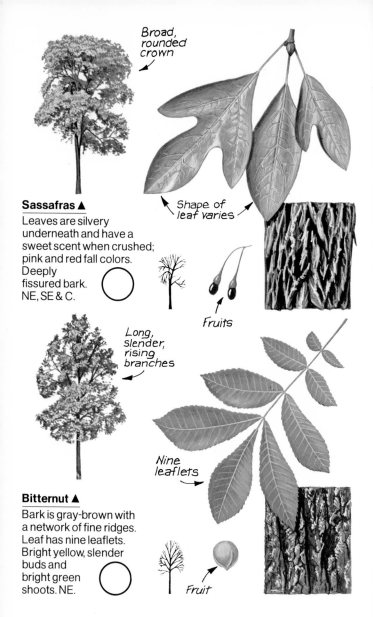

Broad, rounded crown

Shape of leaf varies

Fruits

Sassafras ▲

Leaves are silvery underneath and have a sweet scent when crushed; pink and red fall colors. Deeply fissured bark. NE, SE & C.

Long, slender, rising branches

Nine leaflets

Bitternut ▲

Bark is gray-brown with a network of fine ridges. Leaf has nine leaflets. Bright yellow, slender buds and bright green shoots. NE.

Fruit

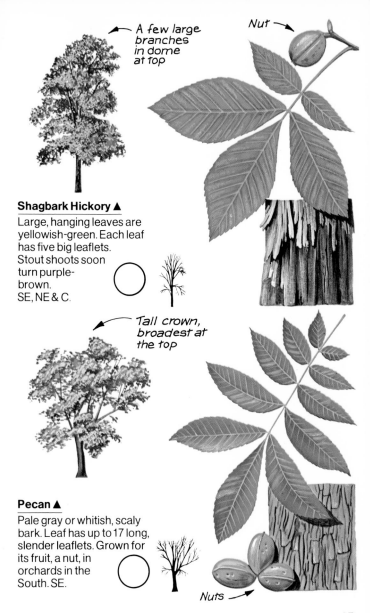

A few large branches in dome at top

Nut →

Shagbark Hickory ▲

Large, hanging leaves are yellowish-green. Each leaf has five big leaflets. Stout shoots soon turn purple-brown.
SE, NE & C.

Tall crown, broadest at the top

Pecan ▲

Pale gray or whitish, scaly bark. Leaf has up to 17 long, slender leaflets. Grown for its fruit, a nut, in orchards in the South. SE.

Nuts →

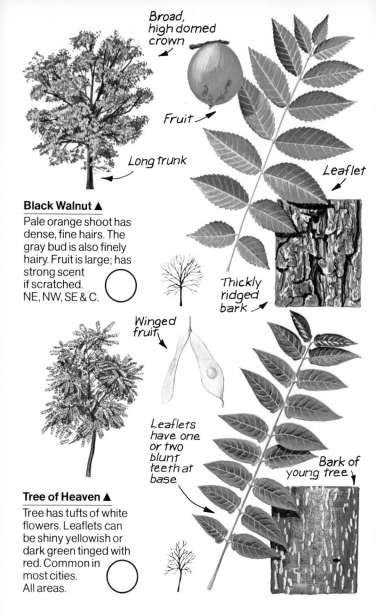

Broad, high domed crown

Fruit

Long trunk

Leaflet

Black Walnut ▲

Pale orange shoot has dense, fine hairs. The gray bud is also finely hairy. Fruit is large; has strong scent if scratched. NE, NW, SE & C.

Thickly ridged bark

Winged fruit

Leaflets have one or two blunt teeth at base

Bark of young tree

Tree of Heaven ▲

Tree has tufts of white flowers. Leaflets can be shiny yellowish or dark green tinged with red. Common in most cities. All areas.

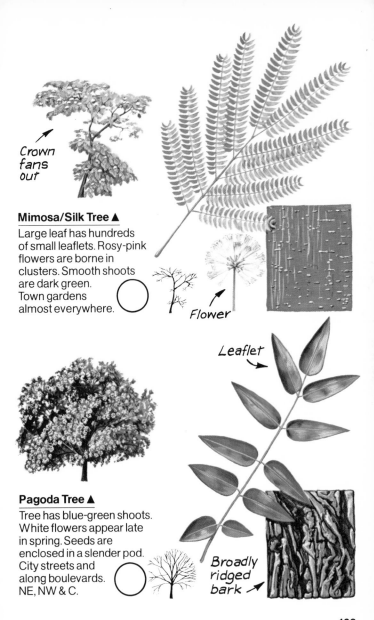

Crown fans out

Mimosa/Silk Tree ▲

Large leaf has hundreds of small leaflets. Rosy-pink flowers are borne in clusters. Smooth shoots are dark green. Town gardens almost everywhere.

Flower

Leaflet

Pagoda Tree ▲

Tree has blue-green shoots. White flowers appear late in spring. Seeds are enclosed in a slender pod. City streets and along boulevards. NE, NW & C.

Broadly ridged bark

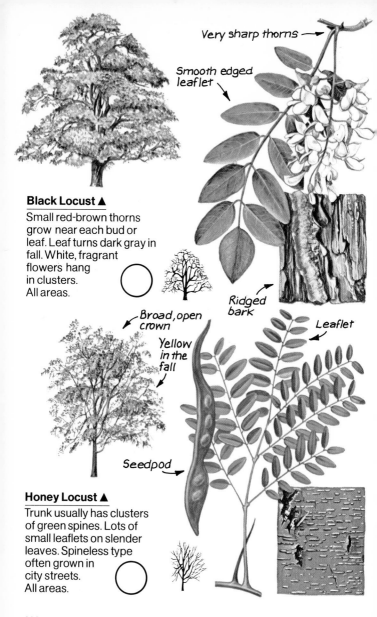

Very sharp thorns →

Smooth edged
leaflet ↘

Black Locust ▲
Small red-brown thorns
grow near each bud or
leaf. Leaf turns dark gray in
fall. White, fragrant
flowers hang
in clusters.
All areas.

Ridged
bark

Broad, open
crown

Yellow
in the
fall

Leaflet

Seedpod

Honey Locust ▲
Trunk usually has clusters
of green spines. Lots of
small leaflets on slender
leaves. Spineless type
often grown in
city streets.
All areas.

110

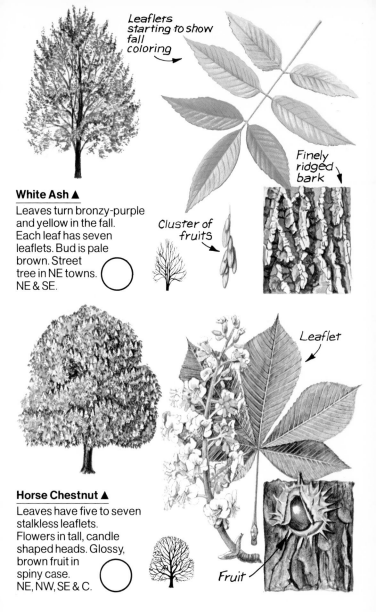

Leaflets starting to show fall coloring

Finely ridged bark

White Ash ▲
Leaves turn bronzy-purple and yellow in the fall. Each leaf has seven leaflets. Bud is pale brown. Street tree in NE towns. NE & SE.

Cluster of fruits

Leaflet

Horse Chestnut ▲
Leaves have five to seven stalkless leaflets. Flowers in tall, candle shaped heads. Glossy, brown fruit in spiny case. NE, NW, SE & C.

Fruit

111

Growing seedlings

Try growing your own tree from a seed. Pick ripe seeds from trees or from the ground. Acorns (oak seeds) and maple seeds are very easy to find, but almost any fresh seed will do. Most seeds take a couple of months to sprout so be patient.

1

Soak the acorns or other hard nuts overnight in warm water. Take the cups off the acorns, but do not try to remove their shells.

2

Put some stones or pebbles in the bottom of a flower pot. This will help the water to drain properly. Fill the pot with soil or compost until the pot is almost full. Place a saucer under the pot and water the soil well.

3

Because the seeds need plenty of room to grow, place only one seed in each pot that you have prepared. Cover the seed with a thin layer of soil. Tamp the soil down to make it firm. Water the soil again lightly.

4

Place a plastic bag over the top of each pot and fasten it with string or a rubber band. This will help to keep the soil inside the pot moist without any watering. Place the pot on a window-sill if possible, or in a sunny place. Wait for the seeds to sprout.

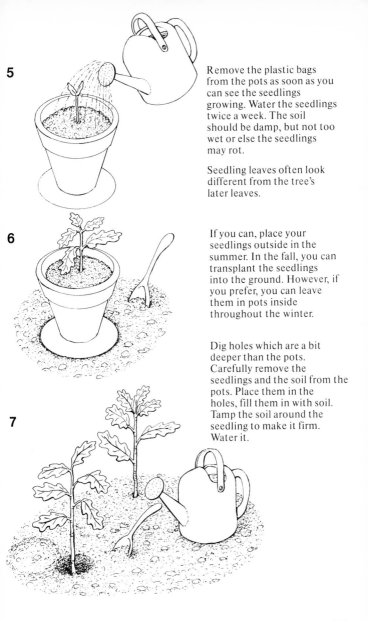

5

Remove the plastic bags from the pots as soon as you can see the seedlings growing. Water the seedlings twice a week. The soil should be damp, but not too wet or else the seedlings may rot.

Seedling leaves often look different from the tree's later leaves.

6

If you can, place your seedlings outside in the summer. In the fall, you can transplant the seedlings into the ground. However, if you prefer, you can leave them in pots inside throughout the winter.

Dig holes which are a bit deeper than the pots. Carefully remove the seedlings and the soil from the pots. Place them in the holes, fill them in with soil. Tamp the soil around the seedling to make it firm. Water it.

7

Winter buds

Most broadleaved trees are deciduous and have no leaves in the winter, but you can identify them by their bark and their winter buds. Conifers have winter buds too, but, since most conifers are evergreen, their needles often hide the buds, making them hard to spot.

Terminal bud

Terminal bud

Scales

Horse Chestnut twig

Spruce twig

Last year's buds were here

Leaf scar

Scale scar

I year's growth

Leaf bud

Scale scar

New twig beginning to grow

Winter buds contain the beginnings of next year's twig, leaves, and flowers. The buds are protected from the winter weather by thick, overlapping scales or by fur. A twig has several buds. All of these buds will become twigs and eventually branches. The terminal (leading) bud contains the shoot that will grow the most; the other buds grow out sideways and are reserves in case the terminal bud is damaged. Each year's growth comes from a bud and ends by making a new bud at the end of the growing season.

If you look at several different trees, you will see that there are many different types of winter buds (see opposite).

How to tell the age of a twig

You can tell how old a twig is by examing the scars left by the buds of previous years. The scales of the terminal bud leave scars that look like tight, tiny rings. The distance between each group of rings shows how much the twig has grown in a given year. If you trace back three or four years, you may notice that in some years the tree grew more than others. This is due, in part, to changing weather conditions and to the amount of water and food the tree had.

Identifying winter buds

Here are the winter buds of some trees which you may see.

White Pine
Pointed orange-brown buds on bright green shoot.

Paper Birch
Slender, green and brown buds on warty, dark brown shoot.

American Elm
Sharp, chestnut-brown bud on light brown shoot.

American Linden
Smooth, bright green, rounded bud on smooth, bright green shoot.

Weeping Willow
Pink to dark red bud has curved tip; shoot is light brown or pale yellow.

Red Oak
Pointed, large, dark brown bud on dark brown shoot, often ribbed.

Buttonwood
Small, brown bud hidden until leaf falls; shoot soon turns shiny brown.

Sugar Maple
Rounded, sharp tipped, scaly bud, dark and pale brown on olive to red-brown shoot.

Black Walnut
Squat, pale brown bud with dense gray hairs on pale brown to orange shoot.

Mimosa
Minute, dark brown bud; dark green, finely ridged shoot with raised warts.

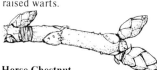

Horse Chestnut
Large, red-brown bud glistening with gummy resin on stout, pink-brown shoot.

Reading tree stumps

Just as twigs and branches reflect the growth of a tree, so does the tree's trunk. You can learn a lot about the life of a tree by reading its "calendar" of annual rings. Every year, a tree grows a ring of new wood. You can see these rings on a freshly cut stump. By counting them you can find out how old the tree is. Some trees, like the Giant Sequoia in California, are thousands of years old. If you know when the tree was cut, you can figure out the year it began to grow or how old it was when you were born. This will only work if the tree was cut near the ground. If it was cut too far above the ground, the earliest rings will not be visible.

Stumps that have been cut recently are the easiest to read. But if you find an old stump, you can rub the top with some sandpaper to make the rings show up more clearly. If you want to make a permanent record of the tree's history, put a strip of white paper on the stump going from the bark into the middle. Then rub lightly with a soft pencil or crayon. The rings will show up on the paper as dark lines.

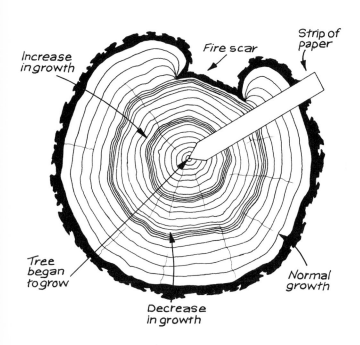

Increase in growth

Fire scar

Strip of paper

Tree began to grow

Normal growth

Decrease in growth

Bark

Trees can also be identified by their bark. The Ponderosa Pine's bark is plated; the American Beech has smooth bark that is grayish; the Shagbark Hickory's bark is shaggy; and the Paper Birch tree has whitish, papery bark that comes off in strips. It is from the Paper Birch that the North American Indians made their famous birch bark canoes.

Ponderosa Pine (plated)   **American Beech (smooth)**   **Shagbark Hickory (shaggy)**   **Paper Birch (papery)**

Bark works like skin. It insulates the tree from heat and cold; and it protects the tree from disease. It also keeps the tree from drying out. Underneath the bark are tubes that carry food (sap) up and down the tree. These tubes can be damaged if the bark is stripped off. If this happens, the tree may die.

Often the bark of a young tree looks different from that of a mature tree. This is because as a tree grows its bark thickens.

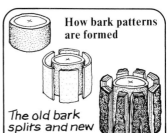

How bark patterns are formed

The old bark splits and new bark forms underneath ▸

Making bark rubbings

Making bark rubbings is quite simple. Just tape a piece of thin, strong paper (white or light-colored) to the tree trunk. Then rub firmly up and down with a soft pencil or crayon until the pattern appears. Be careful not to tear the paper by rubbing too hard.

Pressing leaves

You can make a collection of the leaves you find. To press the leaves, put each one between two sheets of soft, absorbent paper (newspaper or blotting paper would be the best). Then put the sheets under a very heavy book and weight it down some more with something very heavy, like a brick. Don't stack up too many sheets – only about three or four per pile.

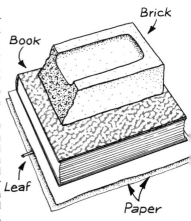

After about a week, when the leaves are flat and dry, you can remove them from the press and paste them in a notebook. Or you can use them for various arts and crafts projects, like a collage, for instance, made with a combination of pressed leaves and other natural objects (grasses, dried seeds, ferns, and so on).

The Shape of Trees

Trees all have different shapes. Some are tall and thin, like the Norway Spruce, and others are vase-shaped like the American Elm. A tree can be identified, in part, by its shape and by the way the branches grow out from its trunk. It is the arrangement of the branches that gives a tree its shape. Winter is a good time to see these shapes.

Other conditions also shape trees, for example the weather. If there is a steady wind in one direction, it can make a tree grow one-sided. If several trees are growing very close together, in a dense forest for example, they will grow quite tall and not branch out till near the top. If a tree grows by itself, it will form a wide crown so that the leaves get plenty of sunlight. People prune trees to get them to grow in special ways.

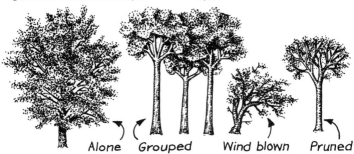

Alone   Grouped   Wind blown   Pruned

Making an album

Why not keep a notebook of trees? You can make a page or more for each tree you spot. Include *when* (the date) you saw the tree and *where* – was it along a road, in the mountains, in a city park, in a field, or in a dense forest? Draw a *picture* of it (or take a photo) to show its shape and the way it grows; paste in a pressed *leaf* (or needle). You can also add a twig showing the tree's winter bud and a bark rubbing that you have made. In the spring you can put in a drawing of the tree's flower and later, in the fall, add one of the fruits or seeds.

If the trees in your album are trees that are near your home, you can keep track of them throughout the year and record their seasonal changes – such as when the flowers bloom and when the leaves begin to change color and fall. You can also keep track of them from year to year. Ask yourself questions. Do the leaves turn at the same time every year? How does the weather affect the tree's processes? What other changes that might affect the tree(s) have taken place?

Sugar Maple
(*Acer saccharum*)

Leaf 11/11/78

Bark rubbing made 11/11/78

Memorial Park 10/10/78

Twig with winter buds 11/11/78

Seed 11/11/78

Flower 5/5/78

Books to read

A Guide to Field Identification; Trees of North America. C. Frank Brockman and Rebecca Merrilees. A Golden Press paperback with color pictures and range maps.
Master Tree Finder. May T. Watts. A small paperback published by the Nature Study Guild. Covers everything east of the Rocky Mountains. Identifies trees by their leaves. A handy pocket guide.
Desert Tree Finder. May T. Watts and Tom Watts. Same format as the *Master Tree Finder.* This guide covers southwestern California, Arizona, and New Mexico.

A Field Guide to Trees and Shrubs. George Petrides. A paperback in the Peterson Field Guide series, published by Houghton Mifflin, Co. Covers northeastern and central North America.
Trees of our National Forests; Their Beauty and Use. U.S. Department of Agriculture. An informative booklet about the National Forests and the major trees found in them.
International Book of Trees. Hugh Johnson. A large hardcover book with color photographs, published by Simon and Schuster. Worth getting out of the library.

Places to visit

Petrified Forest National Park, Arizona.
Joshua Tree National Monument, Twenty-nine Palms, California.
Muir Woods National Monument, Mill Valley, California.
Sequoia National Park, Three Rivers, California.
University of California Botanical Gardens, Berkeley, California.
U.S. National Arboretum, Washington, D.C.
Everglades National Park, Homestead, Florida.
Fairchild Tropical Gardens, Miami, Florida.
Chicago Natural History Museum, Chicago, Illinois.
Morton Arboretum, Lisle, Illinois.
Huntington Arboretum, Muncie, Indiana.
Huntingdon Garden, Los Angeles, California.
Lilly Cornett Woods, Skyline, Kentucky.
Arnold Arboretum, Jamaica Plain (Boston), Massachusetts.

American Museum of Natural History, New York, New York.
Bronx Botanical Gardens, Bronx, New York.
Brooklyn Botanical Gardens, Brooklyn, New York.
Planting Fields Arboretum, Oyster Bay, New York.
Joyce Kilmer Memorial Forest, Robbinsville, North Carolina.
Sara P. Duke Gardens, Durham, North Carolina.
Dysart Woods, Belmont, Ohio.
Longwood Gardens, Kennett Square, Pennsylvania.
Cypress Gardens, Magnolia Gardens, Middleton Place Gardens–all near Charleston, South Carolina.
Great Smoky Mountain National Park, Gatlinburg, Tennessee.
Wind River Experimental Forest, Vancouver, Washington.
Madison Arboretum, Madison, Wisconsin.
Trees for Tomorrow Camp, Eagle River, Wisconsin.

Scorecard

When you have seen and identified a tree, use this scorecard to look up the number of points you have scored.

Before looking up your score, look at the map below to find out which area you have seen the tree in. You will see that North America has been divided into five different areas: Northeast, Southeast, Central, Northwest and Southwest. There is a separate scorecard for each of these areas, and the trees that can be found in each area have been listed in alphabetical order.

A low score (the lowest is 5) means that the tree is common and quite easy to find; the highest score is 25, and the higher the score the rarer the tree in that area.

For instance, the Red Maple is fairly common in the North and Southeast (scores 5), rare in the Central and Northwest areas (scores 25), and not found at all in the Southwest.

When you have found your score, you can either ring it in pencil in the book, or you can keep a record of your score in a notebook, making a note of the date you see the flower. Either way you can add up your total score whenever you like – at the end of each day, week or month.

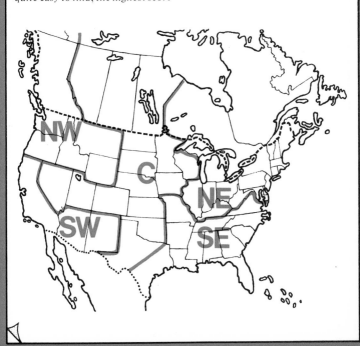

Northeast

This area includes the following states and provinces: Connecticut, Delaware, Illinois, Indiana, Kentucky, Maine, Maryland, Massachusetts, Michigan, New Brunswick, New Hampshire, New Jersey, New York, Newfoundland, Nova Scotia, Ohio, Ontario, Pennsylvania, Quebec, Rhode Island, Vermont, West Virginia.

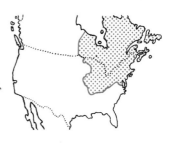

	Score		Score		Score
Ash, White	10	Fir, Balsam	10	Oak, Willow	25
Aspen, Quaking	10	Ginkgo	10	·Pagoda Tree	20
Beech, American	10	Gum, Sweet	15	Pine, Austrian	5
Beech, Purple	20	Hemlock, Eastern	10	Pine, Jeffrey	25
Birch, Paper	10	Hickory, Shagbark	10	Pine, Ponderosa	25
Birch, European White	20	Linden, American	5	Pine, Scots	5
Birch, Swedish	25	Linden, Small-leafed	10	Pine, White	5
Bitternut	20	Maple, Norway	5	Poplar, Balsam	10
Buttonwood	10	Maple, Red	5	Poplar, Lombardy	5
Catalpa	20	Maple, Silver	5	Redwood, Dawn	20
Cedar, Western Red	25	Maple, Sugar	5	Sassafras	20
Cherry, Sweet	20	Mimosa	10	Spruce, Blue Colorado	10
Chestnut, Horse	5	Mulberry, White	20	Spruce, Norway	5
Cottonwood	5	Oak, Burr	15	Tamarack	15
Cypress, Swamp	20	Oak, Pin	15	Tree of Heaven	20
Deodar	25	Oak, Post	25	Tulip Tree	15
Elm, American	5	Oak, Red	5	Walnut, Black	10
Empress Tree	25	Oak, White	10	Willow, Weeping	10

Southeast

This area includes the following states:
Alabama, Arkansas, Florida, Georgia, Louisiana, Mississippi, Missouri, North Carolina, South Carolina, Tennessee, Texas (eastern), Virginia

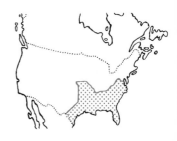

	Score		Score		Score
Ash, White	20	Locust, Black	15	Palmetto, Cabbage	20
Beech, American	5	Locust, Honey	5	Pear, Bradford	20
Buttonwood	5	Magnolia, Southern	5	Pecan	5
Catalpa, Southern	10	Maple, Norway	20	Pine, Loblolly	5
Chestnut, Horse	25	Maple, Red	5	Pine, White	10
Cottonwood	5	Maple, Silver	15	Poplar, Lombardy	5
Cypress, Italian	15	Maple, Sugar	15	Redwood, Dawn	20
Cypress, Swamp	10	Mimosa	5	Sassafras	10
Deodar	10	Mulberry, White	20	Spruce, Blue Colorado	15
Elm, American	5	Oak, Blackjack	5	Spruce, Norway	5
Elm, Siberian	25	Oak, Burr	20	Sugarberry	10
Empress Tree	20	Oak, Live	10	Tallow Tree, Chinese	15
Ginkgo	10	Oak, Pin	10	Tree of Heaven	5
Gum, Sweet	5	Oak, Post	5	Tulip Tree	5
Hemlock, Eastern	10	Oak, Red	15	Walnut, Black	10
Hickory, Shagbark	25	Oak, White	5	Washingtonia, California	25
Linden, American	20	Oak, Willow	5	Washingtonia, Mexican	20
Linden, Small-leafed	25	Palm, Canary	20	Willow, Babylon	10

Central

This area includes the following states and provinces: Alberta, Colorado, Iowa, Kansas, Manitoba, Minnesota, Nebraska, Nevada, North Dakota, Oklahoma, Saskatchewan, South Dakota, Texas (western), Utah, Wisconsin

	Score		Score		Score
Aspen, Quaking	5	Locust, Honey	5	Pine, Limber	15
Beech, Purple	25	Magnolia, Southern	25	Pine, Lodgepole	10
Birch, Paper	20	Maple, Norway	20	Pine, Ponderosa	10
Birch, European White	10	Maple, Red	25	Pine, Scots	15
Birch, Swedish	5	Maple, Silver	10	Pine, White	15
Buttonwood	15	Maple, Sugar	15	Poplar, Balsam	10
Catalpa	20	Mimosa	20	Poplar, Bolle's	10
Chestnut, Horse	5	Mulberry, White	20	Poplar, Lombardy	5
Cottonwood	5	Oak, Blackjack	20	Sassafras	20
Cypress, Swamp	25	Oak, Burr	10	Spruce, Colorado	5
Elm, American	5	Oak, Pin	10	Spruce, Engelmann	10
Elm, Siberian	5	Oak, Post	20	Spruce, Norway	15
Ginkgo	20	Oak, Red	10	Sugarberry	10
Gum, Sweet	20	Oak, White	15	Tamarack	20
Hickory, Shagbark	25	Olive, Russian	15	Tree of Heaven	15
Linden, American	15	Pagoda Tree	25	Walnut, Black	15
Linden, Small-leafed	10	Pear, Bradford	25	Willow, Weeping	10
Locust, Black	20	Pine, Austrian	5		

Northwest

This area includes the following
states and provinces:
British Columbia, Idaho, Montana,
Oregon, Washington, Wyoming

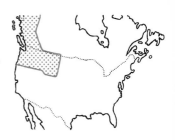

	Score		Score		Score
Aspen, Quaking	15	Hemlock, Western	5	Pine, Ponderosa	5
Ash, White	15	Linden, American	25	Pine, Scots	20
Beech, American	25	Linden, Small-leafed	15	Poplar, Balsam	5
Beech, Purple	20	Locust, Black	5	Poplar, Lombardy	5
Birch, Paper	15	Locust, Honey	10	Redwood, Coast	25
Birch, European White	10	Maple, Norway	20	Redwood, Dawn	25
Birch, Swedish	10	Maple, Oregon	5	Sequoia, Giant	20
Catalpa	20	Maple, Red	25	Spruce, Colorado	10
Cedar, Western Red	5	Maple, Silver	15	Spruce, Engelmann	15
Cherry, Sweet	10	Maple, Sugar	25	Spruce, Norway	15
Chestnut, Horse	5	Mulberry, White	25	Spruce, Sitka	10
Deodar	15	Oak, Pin	20	Sugarberry	15
Elm, American	20	Oak, Red	25	Tree of Heaven	15
Elm, Siberian	25	Pagoda Tree	25	Tulip Tree	20
Empress Tree	25	Pine, Austrian	20	Walnut, Black	25
Fir, Douglas	5	Pine, Jeffrey	20	Willow, Weeping	10
Ginkgo	25	Pine, Limber	25		
Gum, Sweet	15	Pine, Lodgepole	10		

Southwest

This area includes the following states:
Arizona, California, New Mexico

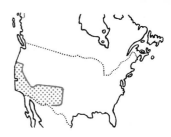

	Score		Score		Score
Aspen, Quaking	20	Olive, Russian	10	Tree of Heaven	10
Birch, European White	5	Palm, Canary	5	Tulip Tree	25
Catalpa, Southern	15	Palmetto, Cabbage	5	Washingtonia, California	5
Cypress, Italian	10	Pine, Aleppo	10	Washingtonia, Mexican	5
Deodar	5	Pine, Canary	10		
Elm, Siberian	5	Pine, Jeffrey	15		
Empress Tree	20	Pine, Limber	25		
Fir, Douglas	15	Pine, Lodgepole	15		
Ginkgo	25	Pine, Ponderosa	5		
Gum, Blue	5	Poplars, Balsam	20		
Gum, Sweet	15	Poplar, Bolle's	20		
Hemlock, Western	20	Poplar, Lombardy	5		
Locust, Black	15	Redwood, Coast	10		
Locust, Honey	10	Redwood, Dawn	20		
Magnolia, Southern	10	Sequoia, Giant	20		
Maple, Silver	15	Spruce, Colorado	10		
Mulberry, White	20	Spruce, Sitka	25		
Nut Pine, Single-leaf	20	Tallow Tree, Chinese	15		

Latin names of trees

Here is a list of the names of the trees in this book, in Latin. The common name of each tree may vary from one area of North America to another, but the Latin name remains the same. It is useful to know for further study.

p. 70 Ginkgo biloba
Taxodium distichum

p. 71 Metasequoia glyptostroboides
Larix laricina

p. 72 Cedrus deodara
Pinus strobus

p. 73 Pinus flexilis
Pinus ponderosa

p. 74 Pinus jeffreyi
Pinus taeda

p. 75 Pinus canariensis
Pinus contorta var. latifolia

p. 76 Pinus sylvestris
Pinus nigra subsp. nigra

p. 77 Pinus halepensis
Pinus cembroides var. monophylla

p. 78 Pseudotsuga menziesii
Tsuga canadensis
Tsuga heterophylla

p. 79 Picea sitchensis
Picea abies

p. 80 Picea pungens var. glauca
Picea engelmanni

p. 81 Sequoiadendron giganteum
Sequoia sempervirens

p. 82 Thuja plicata
Cupressus sempervirens

p. 83 Abies balsamea
Phoenix canariensis

p. 84 Washingtonia filifera
Washingtonia robusta
Sabal palmetto

p. 85 Populus tremuloides
Populus deltoides

p. 86 Populus alba cv. "Pyramidalis"
Populus nigra cv. "Italica"

p. 87 Betula papyrifera
Betula pendula

p. 88 Betula pendula cv. "Dalecarlica"
Ulmus americana

p. 89 Ulmus pumila
Celtis laevigata

p. 90 Sapium sebiferum
Pyrus calleryana cv. "Bradford"

p. 91 Prunus avium
Tilia americana

Part 3
BIRDS

Introduction to Part 3

This section of the book will help you to identify over 170 different species of birds. Birds that are closely related, for example all the gulls, are grouped together.

Here is a list of the birds that are shown on each page:

Identifying birds

This section of the book is an identification guide to some of the birds you will see in North America (both in the USA and Canada). Take it with you when you go looking for birds. The pictures show the birds standing, perching, flying or swimming, depending on how the bird is most often seen.

The male of each kind of bird is always shown. In many cases where the female is very different from the male, the female will be shown too. ♂ means male and ♀ means female. If a bird's plumage (feathers) changes from season to season, both kinds of plumage are shown.

The description next to each bird tells you where to look for it and also gives its approximate average size in inches. The measurements given for most birds are taken from the tip of the beak to the tip of the tail (see diagram). Very long-legged birds such as herons and egrets are measured by their height from head to foot when standing. Birds on the same page are not always drawn to scale.

On the next page you will find a picture showing the different parts of a bird. There is also a list of special words and their meanings on page 189.

Each time you see a bird, check it off in the small circle next to the picture.

Where the birds are found

You can find out the areas of North America in which each bird may be found by looking at the letters at the end of each description; they stand for the following areas:

B = **Both** Eastern and Western regions
E = **Eastern** region
W = **Western** region
N = **North**
S = **South**
NW = **North-West**
NE = **North-East**
SW = **South-West**

Often more than one of these letters will be used: e.g. **B(N)** means that the bird is seen in both Eastern and Western regions, but mostly to the North of those regions; and **E(&SW)** means that the bird is seen in the East and also in the South-West.

Look at the map on page 183 to see how these areas are defined.

Scorecards

There are two scorecards on pages 183-187, one for the Eastern and one for the Western region. You will find a score for each bird you see in either region. You can add up your scores whenever you like, either after a day out spotting birds, or at the end of a vacation, for example.

Where to look for birds

You can start birdwatching in your own backyard or from a window in your home. Try putting out food and water to attract the birds (see pages 180-1 for information and suggestions). When you get to know the birds near your home, you may want to look for different birds. You can look in a nearby park. Ponds, rivers, beaches, fields and woods are all good spots for birdwatching. Even old gravel pits, garbage dumps and swamps attract birds. The best time to go is early in the morning; early evening is also good. If you take a vacation you will be able to visit new places (different habitats) and see new species of birds. When you know the names of some birds you may want to know more about them. There is a list of books to read and clubs to join on page 182.

Binoculars

You do not necessarily need binoculars to watch birds, but as you become more experienced you may want to buy some. Look for a lightweight pair. You should try several types. The best sizes are 7 x 35 or 8 x 40.

Notebook

It is a good idea to keep a notebook. In it you can record the birds you see. Describe (or draw) new birds. This will help you to identify them later.

Parts of a bird's body

These words will help you when you are reading the descriptions in this and other books about birds.

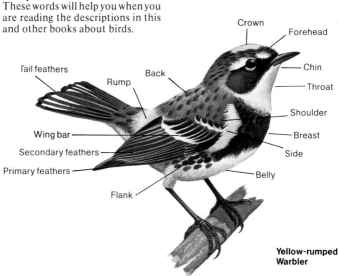

Crown
Forehead
Tail feathers
Back
Chin
Rump
Throat
Shoulder
Breast
Wing bar
Side
Secondary feathers
Primary feathers
Belly
Flank

Yellow-rumped Warbler

Loon, Grebe, Pelican, Gannet

Common Loon ▶

Breeds by inland waters
of Canada and Alaska;
winters on all coasts of
North America. Flies with
neck sloping down. Listen
for eerie,
laughing call.
32″. B.

Summer

Winter

Seldom flies

Floats
high in
water

◀ Pied-billed Grebe

Found on shallow inland
waters. Dives frequently.
When alarmed, sinks
slowly instead
of diving.
13″. B.

Brown Pelican ▶

Seen on coastal waters,
mainly in the south.
Flocks fly in lines. Dives
from flight for fish. Young
are pale brown
all over.
50″. SE & W.

Neck is
white in
winter

Has
powerful
flight with
frequent
short
glides

Often glides on
long, narrow
wings

◀ Gannet

Eastern bird seen on
rocky offshore islands.
Fishes by plunging into
sea from up to 50′ high.
Young are dark
gray with white
spots. 37″. E.

Cormorant, Swan, Egrets

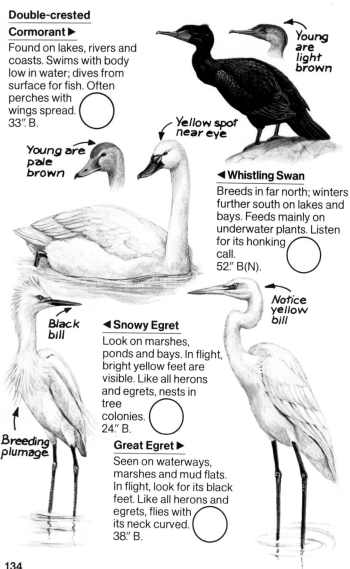

Double-crested
Cormorant ▶
Found on lakes, rivers and coasts. Swims with body low in water; dives from surface for fish. Often perches with wings spread. 33". B.

Young are light brown

Yellow spot near eye

Young are pale brown

◀ Whistling Swan
Breeds in far north; winters further south on lakes and bays. Feeds mainly on underwater plants. Listen for its honking call. 52". B(N).

Black bill

Notice yellow bill

◀ Snowy Egret
Look on marshes, ponds and bays. In flight, bright yellow feet are visible. Like all herons and egrets, nests in tree colonies. 24". B.

Breeding plumage

Great Egret ▶
Seen on waterways, marshes and mud flats. In flight, look for its black feet. Like all herons and egrets, flies with its neck curved. 38". B.

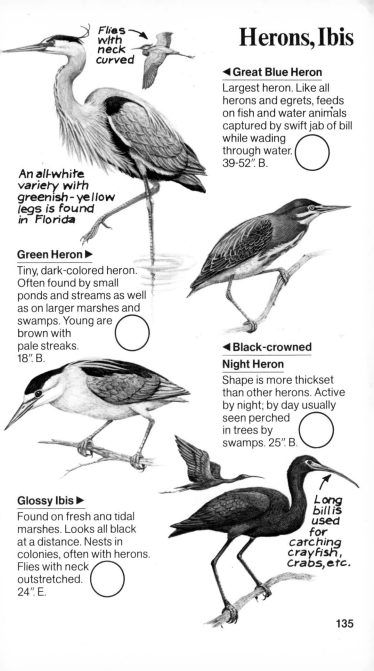

Flies with neck curved

Herons, Ibis

◄ Great Blue Heron

Largest heron. Like all herons and egrets, feeds on fish and water animals captured by swift jab of bill while wading through water. 39-52". B.

An all-white variety with greenish-yellow legs is found in Florida

Green Heron ►

Tiny, dark-colored heron. Often found by small ponds and streams as well as on larger marshes and swamps. Young are brown with pale streaks. 18". B.

◄ Black-crowned
Night Heron

Shape is more thickset than other herons. Active by night; by day usually seen perched in trees by swamps. 25". B.

Glossy Ibis ►

Found on fresh and tidal marshes. Looks all black at a distance. Nests in colonies, often with herons. Flies with neck outstretched. 24". E.

Long bill is used for catching crayfish, crabs, etc.

Geese

Brant

Canada Goose ▶

Several races, varying in size; some have darker bodies than others. Loud, honking call. Flocks fly in V-formation. Feeds in fields near water. 22-45". B.

Brant ▶

Feeds on the shore in bays and estuaries. Flocks fly in wavering lines. 17". E.

Canada Goose

◀ White-fronted Goose

Habits similar to Canada Goose, but nests only in the far north. Has a high-pitched, "yodelling" call. 28". B(W).

White belly

Orange legs

Blue Goose

Snow Goose

Snow Goose ▶

Breeds in Arctic; winters mainly on coastal bays and salt marshes. High pitched, barking call.

Blue Goose ▶

A darker bodied variety, seen mainly in the west and on Gulf coast; both forms may be seen together in mixed flocks. 26". B.

Black wing-tips show in flight

136

Ducks

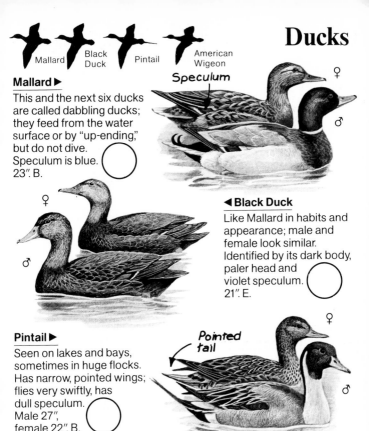

Mallard   Black Duck   Pintail   American Wigeon

Speculum

Mallard ▶

This and the next six ducks are called dabbling ducks; they feed from the water surface or by "up-ending," but do not dive. Speculum is blue. 23". B.

◀ Black Duck

Like Mallard in habits and appearance; male and female look similar. Identified by its dark body, paler head and violet speculum. 21". E.

Pintail ▶

Seen on lakes and bays, sometimes in huge flocks. Has narrow, pointed wings; flies very swiftly, has dull speculum. Male 27", female 22". B.

Pointed tail

◀ American Wigeon

Found on lakes and estuaries; sometimes grazes on land. Has whistling call. Short, stubby bill. Large, white shoulder patches show in flight. 21". B.

Ducks

Northern Shoveler

Blue-winged Teal

Wood Duck

Canvas-back

◀ Northern Shoveler

Feeds on tiny water animals, filtered out by the comblike edges of its huge bill. Bill is noticeable even at a distance. 19″. B.

Blue-winged Teal ▶

In flight, coloring of wings similar to Shoveler, but smaller and shorter billed. Flies in small, densely packed groups. 15″. B.

◀ Wood Duck

Flies swiftly among trees in wooded areas near freshwater. Nests in treeholes; ducklings drop to ground when hatched. 19″. B(E).

Canvasback ▶

This and the next four species feed underwater by diving from water surface. Note Canvasback's flattened head. 21″. B.

Ducks

Lesser Scaup Bufflehead Ruddy Duck Red-breasted Merganser

Lesser Scaup ▶

Very similar to **Greater Scaup,** but Lesser has purple- rather than greenish-glossed head and a higher forehead. Seen on salt and freshwater. 17". B.

♀
♂

◀ Bufflehead

Seen on wooded waterways in summer, coasts in winter. Nests in tree hollows or old woodpecker holes. Dives frequently. 14". B.

♀
♂

Ruddy Duck ▶

Seen on lakes and ponds; estuaries in winter. Wings are shorter and more rounded than in most ducks. 15". B.

♀
♂

♀
♂

◀ Red-breasted Merganser

Seen by rivers and streams in summer, coasts in winter. Flies with head and neck extended in straight line. 23". B.

Jaeger, Gulls

Parasitic Jaeger ▶

Chases other seabirds, especially terns, across open sea, forcing them to drop food, which it then steals. Sometimes seen near coasts. 21". B.

Some individuals are dark brown all over

◀ Great Black-backed Gull

Largest of all gulls. Seen mainly on coastal beaches and lagoons, rarely on inland waters. Young are brown and white. 30". E.

Herring Gull ▶

Found on coasts, lakes and rivers. Often feeds off garbage dumps. Note pink feet and black wing-tips with white spots. 25". B.

◀ Ring-billed Gull

Look for narrow black ring around bill. Often seen inland. Young are mottled brown, tail white with narrow black band near tip. 19". B.

Laughing Gull ▶

Distinguished from other gulls with black heads by its all-dark wing-tips. Seen near coasts. Has a high, laughing call. 16". E.

Terns, Skimmer

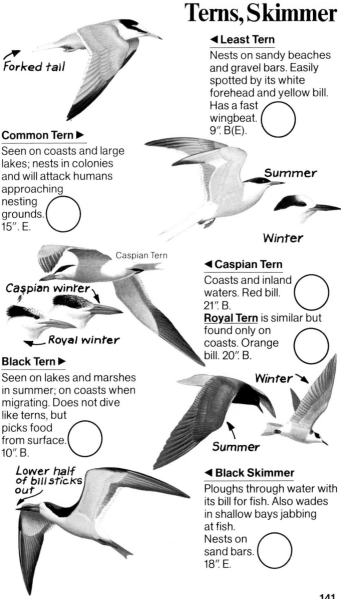

Forked tail

◄ Least Tern
Nests on sandy beaches and gravel bars. Easily spotted by its white forehead and yellow bill. Has a fast wingbeat. 9". B(E).

Common Tern ►
Seen on coasts and large lakes; nests in colonies and will attack humans approaching nesting grounds. 15". E.

Caspian Tern

Caspian winter

Royal winter

Summer

Winter

◄ Caspian Tern
Coasts and inland waters. Red bill. 21". B.
Royal Tern is similar but found only on coasts. Orange bill. 20". B.

Black Tern ►
Seen on lakes and marshes in summer; on coasts when migrating. Does not dive like terns, but picks food from surface. 10". B.

Winter ►

Summer

Lower half of bill sticks out

◄ Black Skimmer
Ploughs through water with its bill for fish. Also wades in shallow bays jabbing at fish. Nests on sand bars. 18". E.

Auks

◀ Razorbill
Breeds on cliff ledges and in crevices. Note the very deep bill, flattened at sides. In winter the throat is white. 17″. NE.

Common Murre ▶
Breeds on rocky ledges; lays pear shaped egg that rolls in a circle not over edge. 17″. B(N).

Thick-billed Murre
is very similar. 18″. B(N).

Thick-billed Murre

Common Murre

Tufted Puffin

Common Puffin

◀ Tufted Puffin
Usually seen on Pacific sea cliffs. When in flight watch it use its webbed feet as brakes. Nests in burrows. 12″ NW.

◀ Common Puffin
Found along Atlantic coast. Has white underparts and no tuft. 12″. NE.

Cassin's Auklet ▶
Seen offshore along Pacific coast, appearing all dark while swimming but pale belly is visible in flight. 7″. W.

Birds of Prey

Black Vulture

White wing-tips

Short tail

Turkey Vulture

◄ **Black Vulture**
Fast wingbeat.
23″. B(S).

◄ **Turkey Vulture**
Soars in wide circles,
rolling and swaying as it
looks for dead birds and
mammals. Nests in hollow
trees or in rock
crevices.
28″. B.

Sharp-shinned Hawk ►
A small hawk, with short,
broad wings and a long
tail. Hunts small birds
along woodland edges
and in thickets.
Nests in conifers.
12″. B.

♂

Female larger

Female and young are brown above instead of gray

♂

◄ **Marsh Hawk**
Glides low over ground,
its long, rounded wings
allowing it to fly very slowly
as it looks for prey. Nests
on ground in
marshes.
20″. B.

Birds of Prey

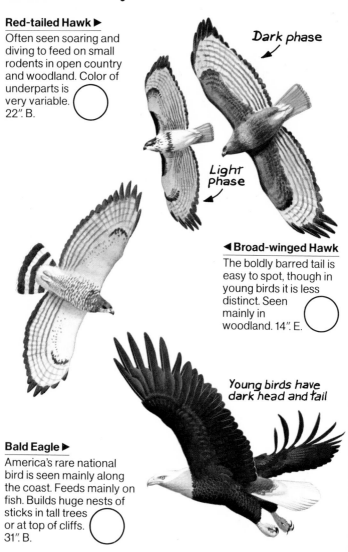

Red-tailed Hawk ▶
Often seen soaring and
diving to feed on small
rodents in open country
and woodland. Color of
underparts is
very variable.
22″. B.

Dark phase

Light phase

◀ Broad-winged Hawk
The boldly barred tail is
easy to spot, though in
young birds it is less
distinct. Seen
mainly in
woodland. 14″. E.

*Young birds have
dark head and tail*

Bald Eagle ▶
America's rare national
bird is seen mainly along
the coast. Feeds mainly on
fish. Builds huge nests of
sticks in tall trees
or at top of cliffs.
31″. B.

Birds of Prey, Game Birds

Osprey ▶
Large, long winged sea hawk with noticeable bend in wing. Hovers over fish and catches them with talons. 23". B.

Dark brown line ↓

Body is dark brown above ↑

Rusty tail and back →

◀ American Kestrel
Seen in countryside and cities, often near highways. Feeds on insects, rodents and small birds. Seeks prey while hovering. 8½". B.

Turkey ▶
Wild ancestor of the familiar domestic bird. Seen in open woodland clearings. Male is 48"; female is 36". E(S).

◀ Spruce Grouse
Look for the distinctive tail pattern and flanks spotted white. Nests on ground in spruce forests. Cry is a deep hoot. 16". B(N).

Game Birds

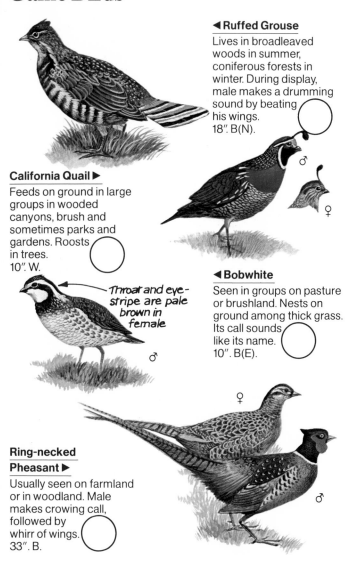

◀ Ruffed Grouse
Lives in broadleaved woods in summer, coniferous forests in winter. During display, male makes a drumming sound by beating his wings. 18″. B(N).

California Quail ▶
Feeds on ground in large groups in wooded canyons, brush and sometimes parks and gardens. Roosts in trees. 10″. W.

Throat and eye-stripe are pale brown in female

♂

◀ Bobwhite
Seen in groups on pasture or brushland. Nests on ground among thick grass. Its call sounds like its name. 10″. B(E).

Ring-necked Pheasant ▶
Usually seen on farmland or in woodland. Male makes crowing call, followed by whirr of wings. 33″. B.

Crane, Rails

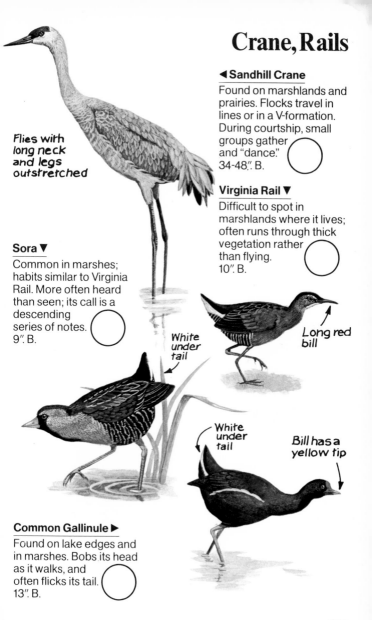

◄ Sandhill Crane
Found on marshlands and prairies. Flocks travel in lines or in a V-formation. During courtship, small groups gather and "dance." 34-48". B.

Virginia Rail ▼
Difficult to spot in marshlands where it lives; often runs through thick vegetation rather than flying. 10". B.

Flies with long neck and legs outstretched

Sora ▼
Common in marshes; habits similar to Virginia Rail. More often heard than seen; its call is a descending series of notes. 9". B.

Long red bill

White under tail

White under tail

Bill has a yellow tip

Common Gallinule ►
Found on lake edges and in marshes. Bobs its head as it walks, and often flicks its tail. 13". B.

Coot, Shorebirds

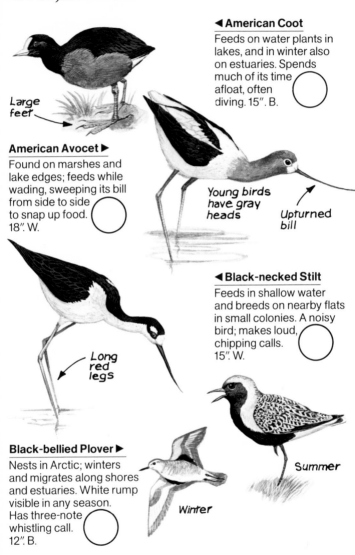

◄ American Coot
Feeds on water plants in lakes, and in winter also on estuaries. Spends much of its time afloat, often diving. 15". B.

American Avocet ►
Found on marshes and lake edges; feeds while wading, sweeping its bill from side to side to snap up food. 18". W.

Young birds have gray heads

Upturned bill

Large feet

◄ Black-necked Stilt
Feeds in shallow water and breeds on nearby flats in small colonies. A noisy bird; makes loud, chipping calls. 15". W.

Long red legs

Black-bellied Plover ►
Nests in Arctic; winters and migrates along shores and estuaries. White rump visible in any season. Has three-note whistling call. 12". B.

Winter

Summer

Shorebirds

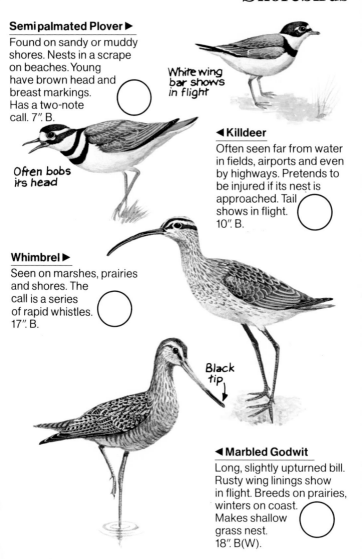

Semipalmated Plover ►
Found on sandy or muddy shores. Nests in a scrape on beaches. Young have brown head and breast markings. Has a two-note call. 7". B.

White wing bar shows in flight

Often bobs its head

◄ Killdeer
Often seen far from water in fields, airports and even by highways. Pretends to be injured if its nest is approached. Tail shows in flight. 10". B.

Whimbrel ►
Seen on marshes, prairies and shores. The call is a series of rapid whistles. 17". B.

Black tip

◄ Marbled Godwit
Long, slightly upturned bill. Rusty wing linings show in flight. Breeds on prairies, winters on coast. Makes shallow grass nest. 18". B(W).

Shorebirds

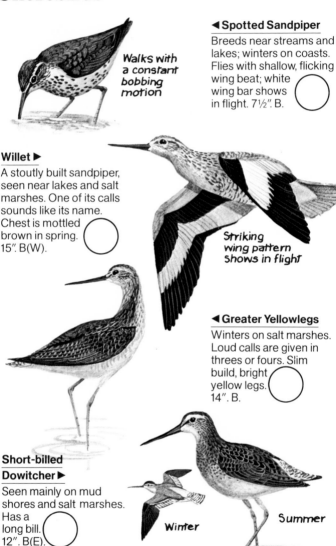

Walks with a constant bobbing motion

◄ **Spotted Sandpiper**
Breeds near streams and lakes; winters on coasts. Flies with shallow, flicking wing beat; white wing bar shows in flight. 7½". B.

Willet ►
A stoutly built sandpiper, seen near lakes and salt marshes. One of its calls sounds like its name. Chest is mottled brown in spring. 15". B(W).

Striking wing pattern shows in flight

◄ **Greater Yellowlegs**
Winters on salt marshes. Loud calls are given in threes or fours. Slim build, bright yellow legs. 14". B.

Short-billed Dowitcher ►
Seen mainly on mud shores and salt marshes. Has a long bill. 12". B(E).

Winter

Summer

Shorebirds

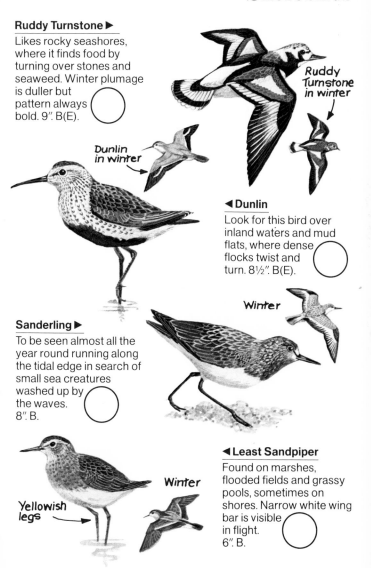

Ruddy Turnstone ▶
Likes rocky seashores, where it finds food by turning over stones and seaweed. Winter plumage is duller but pattern always bold. 9″. B(E).

Ruddy Turnstone in winter

Dunlin in winter

◀ Dunlin
Look for this bird over inland waters and mud flats, where dense flocks twist and turn. 8½″. B(E).

Winter

Sanderling ▶
To be seen almost all the year round running along the tidal edge in search of small sea creatures washed up by the waves. 8″. B.

◀ Least Sandpiper
Found on marshes, flooded fields and grassy pools, sometimes on shores. Narrow white wing bar is visible in flight. 6″. B.

Winter

Yellowish legs

Shorebirds, Woodcock, Snipe

Has stouter bill than Least Sandpiper

Black legs

Winter →

◄ Semipalmated Sandpiper
Seen mainly on shore or at river and lake edges; forms large flocks on migration. Its feet are partly webbed. 6½". E.

Notice wing stripe →

Northern Phalarope ►
Swims floating high on water, sometimes spinning to disturb prey. Breeds near inland pools but winters at sea. 7". B(W).

Summer
♀

Plumage looks like leaves →

◄ American Woodcock
Active mainly at night. Difficult to see in damp woodlands where it lives because of its good camouflage coloring. 11". E.

Common Snipe ►
Prefers swampland, pools and ditches. When disturbed, rises with harsh call and flies away in zigzags. Nests in damp meadows, marshes. 11". B.

Pigeon, Doves, Cuckoos

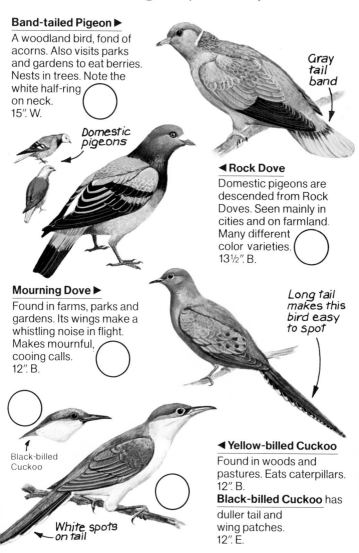

Band-tailed Pigeon ▶
A woodland bird, fond of acorns. Also visits parks and gardens to eat berries. Nests in trees. Note the white half-ring on neck.
15". W.

Gray tail band

Domestic pigeons

◀ Rock Dove
Domestic pigeons are descended from Rock Doves. Seen mainly in cities and on farmland. Many different color varieties.
13½". B.

Mourning Dove ▶
Found in farms, parks and gardens. Its wings make a whistling noise in flight. Makes mournful, cooing calls.
12". B.

Long tail makes this bird easy to spot

Black-billed Cuckoo

◀ Yellow-billed Cuckoo
Found in woods and pastures. Eats caterpillars.
12". B.
Black-billed Cuckoo has duller tail and wing patches.
12". E.

White spots on tail

Roadrunner, Owls

Roadrunner ▶
Large ground living cuckoo of deserts and dry bushland. Runs rapidly after prey such as lizards and snakes. 22". W.

Bushy crest

Gray phase

Red phase

◀ Screech Owl
Found in woods, gardens and orchards. Nests in tree hollows. May attack humans who come too near. Gray, brown and reddish color phases (varieties) occur. 10". B.

Great Horned Owl ▶
Found in all types of habitat, including parks and gardens. Nests on cliff ledges or in old nests of hawks or crows. 25". B.

Owls, Whip-poor-will, Nighthawk

Barred Owl ▶
Found in damp woods and swamp forests. Roosts in tree foliage and comes out at night to seek prey. Usually nests in tree hollows.
20". E.

 Dark eyes

◀ Saw-whet Owl
Found in conifers and other evergreens. Very tame if approached at roosting place in daylight. Eats small rodents.
7". B.

Whip-poor-will ▶
Found on woodland edges. Almost invisible on ground because of camouflaged plumage. Active at night; catches insects in flight.
10". E(& SW).

Wings more pointed than Whip-poor-will's

◀ Common Nighthawk
Found in cities and open country. Active mostly in early evening; also seen in daytime and at night. Often nests on roofs.
10". B.

Swift, Hummingbirds

Short tail →

◄ Chimney Swift

Always on the wing, except when at nest on wall of cave or chimney. Narrower wings than Swallow. 5½". E

Ruby-throated Hummingbird ►

Hovers over flowers to feed on nectar. Wings beat so fast they are invisible and make a humming sound. 3½". E.

Male has red throat

♂

♀

◄ Black-chinned Hummingbird

Found in many habitats; will visit special hummingbird feeders in gardens. 3½". W.

♂

Female has white throat

Rufous Hummingbird ►

Found in many habitats, including woodlands. Female is less brightly colored than male. Builds a tiny nest on tree branch. 4". W.

Female has black and white tail

♂

Kingfisher, Woodpeckers

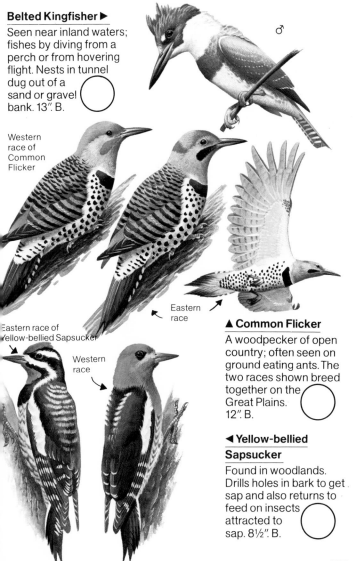

Belted Kingfisher ▶

Seen near inland waters; fishes by diving from a perch or from hovering flight. Nests in tunnel dug out of a sand or gravel bank. 13″. B.

♂

Western race of Common Flicker

Eastern race

Eastern race of Yellow-bellied Sapsucker

Western race

▲ Common Flicker

A woodpecker of open country; often seen on ground eating ants. The two races shown breed together on the Great Plains. 12″. B.

◀ Yellow-bellied Sapsucker

Found in woodlands. Drills holes in bark to get sap and also returns to feed on insects attracted to sap. 8½″. B.

Woodpeckers, Flycatchers

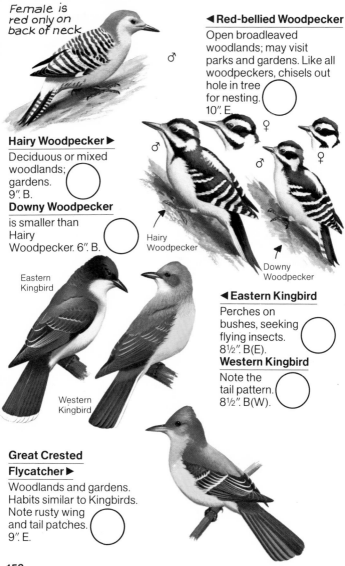

Female is red only on back of neck

♂

◄ Red-bellied Woodpecker

Open broadleaved woodlands; may visit parks and gardens. Like all woodpeckers, chisels out hole in tree for nesting. 10″. E.

♀

♂

♀

Hairy Woodpecker ►

Deciduous or mixed woodlands; gardens. 9″. B.

Downy Woodpecker

is smaller than Hairy Woodpecker. 6″. B.

Hairy Woodpecker

Downy Woodpecker

Eastern Kingbird

◄ Eastern Kingbird

Perches on bushes, seeking flying insects. 8½″. B(E).

Western Kingbird

Note the tail pattern. 8½″. B(W).

Western Kingbird

Great Crested Flycatcher ►

Woodlands and gardens. Habits similar to Kingbirds. Note rusty wing and tail patches. 9″. E.

Flycatchers, Lark

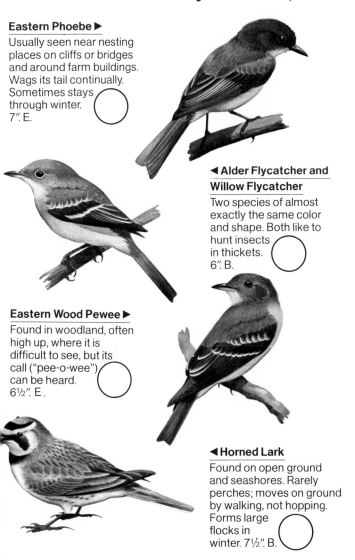

Eastern Phoebe ▶

Usually seen near nesting places on cliffs or bridges and around farm buildings. Wags its tail continually. Sometimes stays through winter. 7". E.

◀ Alder Flycatcher and Willow Flycatcher

Two species of almost exactly the same color and shape. Both like to hunt insects in thickets. 6". B.

Eastern Wood Pewee ▶

Found in woodland, often high up, where it is difficult to see, but its call ("pee-o-wee") can be heard. 6½". E.

◀ Horned Lark

Found on open ground and seashores. Rarely perches; moves on ground by walking, not hopping. Forms large flocks in winter. 7½". B.

Swallows

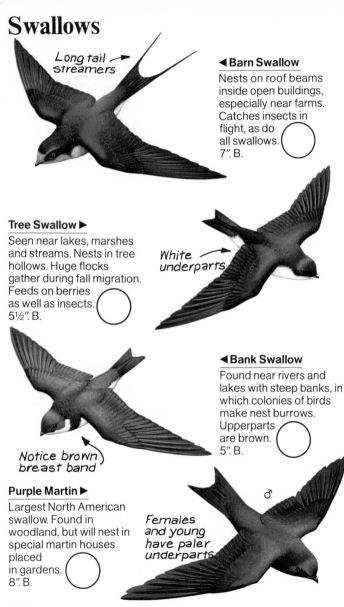

Long tail streamers →

◄ Barn Swallow
Nests on roof beams inside open buildings, especially near farms. Catches insects in flight, as do all swallows. 7". B.

Tree Swallow ►
Seen near lakes, marshes and streams. Nests in tree hollows. Huge flocks gather during fall migration. Feeds on berries as well as insects. 5½". B.

White underparts →

◄ Bank Swallow
Found near rivers and lakes with steep banks, in which colonies of birds make nest burrows. Upperparts are brown. 5". B.

Notice brown breast band

Purple Martin ►
Largest North American swallow. Found in woodland, but will nest in special martin houses placed in gardens. 8". B.

♂

Females and young have paler underparts

Jays, Magpies

◄ Blue Jay
Found in deciduous and mixed woods; parks, gardens and backyards in suburbs. Fond of oak trees. Builds a stick nest in the fork of a tree. 12". E.

Steller's Jay ►
Prefers conifers and mixed woods for nesting. Moves to oak woods in winter. Like the Blue Jay, imitates Hawks. 13". W.

Yellow-billed Magpie

Black-billed Magpie

◄ Black-billed Magpie
Prefers open country with bushes in which it makes large domed nest. 20". B.

Yellow-billed Magpie
nests in colonies. 17". W.

Raven, Crow, Chickadee, Titmouse

Look for its wedge shaped tail in flight

Pointed throat feathers

◀ **Common Raven**
Found in mountainous areas, deserts and northern forests. Its deep, throaty call is quite different from the Crow's. 24″. W (rarely E).

Common Crow ▶
Common almost everywhere, in countryside or cities. Builds stick nest in trees, often in colonies. Roosts in groups. 19″. B.

◀ **Black-capped Chickadee**
Moves acrobatically among twigs and branches while feeding in woods and at garden bird feeders. Nests in hollow in rotten wood. 5″. B.

Tufted Titmouse ▶
Similar habits to Chickadee, but rather more shy. In Texas, crest is black, in other areas gray. 6″. E.

Dipper, Nuthatches, Creeper

Dipper ▶
Looks like a giant wren. Found by swift-flowing rivers; often perches on rock, bobbing. Moves with ease underwater to find food. 8″. W.

◀ White-breasted Nuthatch
Seen in broadleaved woods, climbing trees to find food in bark. Nests in tree holes. Visits bird feeders. 5½″. B.

Red-breasted Nuthatch ▶
Seen in coniferous woods. Habits similar to White-breasted, but visits gardens less and is shyer. 4½″. B.

Climbs downward head first

◀ Brown Creeper
Like Nuthatches, feeds from bark, but usually climbs upward, supporting itself on stiff tail feathers. Nests behind loose bark or in ivy. 5½″. B.

Wrens, Mockingbird

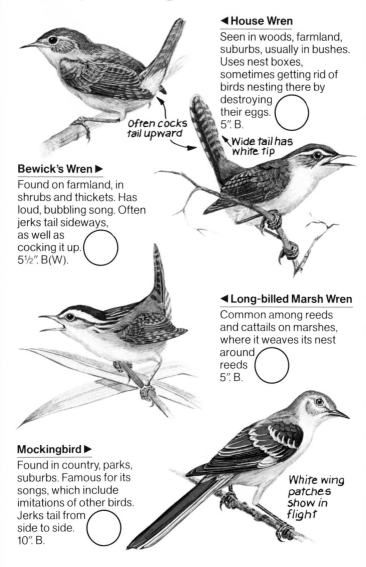

Often cocks tail upward

◀ House Wren
Seen in woods, farmland, suburbs, usually in bushes. Uses nest boxes, sometimes getting rid of birds nesting there by destroying their eggs. 5". B.

Wide tail has white tip

Bewick's Wren ▶
Found on farmland, in shrubs and thickets. Has loud, bubbling song. Often jerks tail sideways, as well as cocking it up. 5½". B(W).

◀ Long-billed Marsh Wren
Common among reeds and cattails on marshes, where it weaves its nest around reeds 5". B.

Mockingbird ▶
Found in country, parks, suburbs. Famous for its songs, which include imitations of other birds. Jerks tail from side to side. 10". B.

White wing patches show in flight

Mockingbirds, Robin, Thrush

Gray Catbird ▶
Often seen in dense thickets. Has a mewing call. Often flicks its tail to show rusty patch under tail. 8½". B.

Black cap

◀ Brown Thrasher
Found in thickets, scrub and woodland edges. Often feeds on ground among dead leaves. Song similar to Mockingbird's. Looks rather thrushlike. 11½". E.

American Robin ▶
Familiar bird of woods and gardens, usually seen hunting worms on lawns. Its mud and grass nest is often placed against a building. 10". B.

Young have paler, spotted underparts

Rusty back

◀ Wood Thrush
Found in woods and gardens, usually damp ones. Spots on breast are larger than on other thrushes. Sings at night as well as during day. 8". E.

165

Thrushes, Kinglet

◄ Hermit Thrush
A woodland bird, often seen under thick cover, looking for food. Has beautiful song. Slowly raises and lowers tail while perched. 7". B.

Rusty tail but dull back

Veery ►
Look in damp woodlands and willow thickets. Has less spotting on underparts than Wood and Hermit Thrushes. Rather shy. 7". B.

Rusty back

Female is duller; young are spotted

◄ Eastern Bluebird
Perches rather upright, watching for insects.
Western Bluebird is similar but has rusty patch on back. Both 7".

Mountain Bluebird ►
Breeds in meadows at high altitudes. Winters at lower altitudes. Sings at dawn. 7". W.

◄ Golden-crowned Kinglet
Hunts insects among conifer branches. Nest hangs from conifer twigs. 4". B.

Waxwing, Starling, Vireos

Cedar Waxwing ▶

Can be seen nearly all year in wandering flocks which feed on berry-bearing bushes. Can store berries in a pouch near its throat.
7". B.

◀ Starling

Noisy bird, common in town and country. Walks on ground, rather than hopping. Nests in tree hollows and on buildings.
8". B.

White "spectacles" around eyes

Solitary Vireo ▶

Lives in mixed or coniferous woodland. A tame bird. Like other vireos, feeds on insects while moving slowly through trees.
5½". B.

◀ Red-eyed Vireo

Common bird of deciduous forests. Young birds have brown, not red, eyes, but still show the pale eye stripe. Nest hangs from forked twig.
6". B.

Warblers

The warblers on these pages are shown in their spring plumage. In fall, their plumage changes and makes them more difficult to identify.

◀ Black-and-white Warbler

Creeps along tree trunks looking for food, rather like Nuthatch. Seen mainly in deciduous woods; in gardens and parks on migration. 5". B.

Yellow-rumped Warbler ▶

Seen in spruce forests, and on coasts during migration. Western birds have yellow throats; Eastern birds have white throats. Nests in conifers. 5½". B.

Eastern race

◀ Northern Parula

Found in woodland, often near swamps; prefers conifers. Builds its nest inside tufts of spanish moss or lichens on tree limbs. 4½". E.

Yellow Warbler ▶

Look in willow thickets, orchards and gardens. Cup shaped nest is placed in the fork of a sapling. Has yellow spots on tail. 5". B.

Warblers

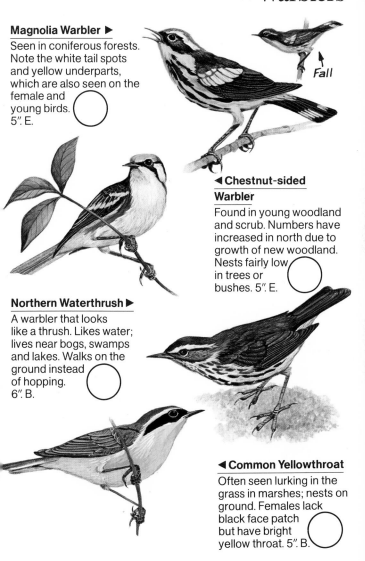

Magnolia Warbler ▶
Seen in coniferous forests. Note the white tail spots and yellow underparts, which are also seen on the female and young birds. 5". E.

Fall

◀ Chestnut-sided Warbler
Found in young woodland and scrub. Numbers have increased in north due to growth of new woodland. Nests fairly low in trees or bushes. 5". E.

Northern Waterthrush ▶
A warbler that looks like a thrush. Likes water; lives near bogs, swamps and lakes. Walks on the ground instead of hopping. 6". B.

◀ Common Yellowthroat
Often seen lurking in the grass in marshes; nests on ground. Females lack black face patch but have bright yellow throat. 5". B.

Warblers, Blackbirds

Female has no black cap

◄ Wilson's Warbler

Fond of willow scrub and thickets of alder near streams. Often seen chasing after flying insects. Nests in weed clumps. 5″. B.

American Redstart ►

Chases flying insects; often fans its tail after a chase. Found in woods and thickets. Nests in the fork of young trees or shrubs. 5″. B.

Female is greenish brown with yellow wing and tail patches

◄ Buff crown stripe

♀

♂

◄ Bobolink

Found in marshes, fields; sometimes in large flocks. Listen for its bubbling, flight song. Makes its nest on the ground. Short bill. 7″. B.

Notice yellow cheeks

Western

Eastern

Eastern/Western
Meadowlark ►

Lives in grasslands; often seen perched on fence posts and telephone wires, singing. Nests in grass. Both 10″.

Blackbirds, Oriole

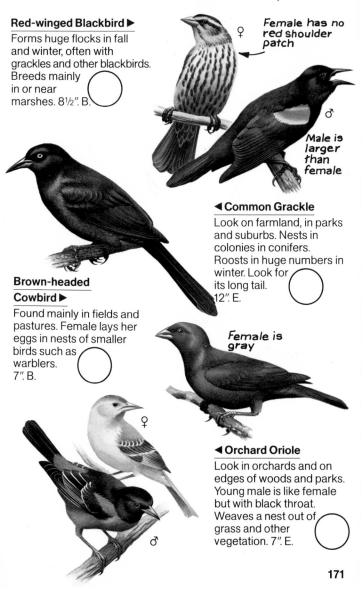

Red-winged Blackbird ▶

Forms huge flocks in fall and winter, often with grackles and other blackbirds. Breeds mainly in or near marshes. 8½". B.

♀ Female has no red shoulder patch

♂ Male is larger than female

◀ Common Grackle

Look on farmland, in parks and suburbs. Nests in colonies in conifers. Roosts in huge numbers in winter. Look for its long tail. 12". E.

Brown-headed Cowbird ▶

Found mainly in fields and pastures. Female lays her eggs in nests of smaller birds such as warblers. 7". B.

Female is gray

◀ Orchard Oriole

Look in orchards and on edges of woods and parks. Young male is like female but with black throat. Weaves a nest out of grass and other vegetation. 7". E.

Orioles, Tanagers, Cardinal

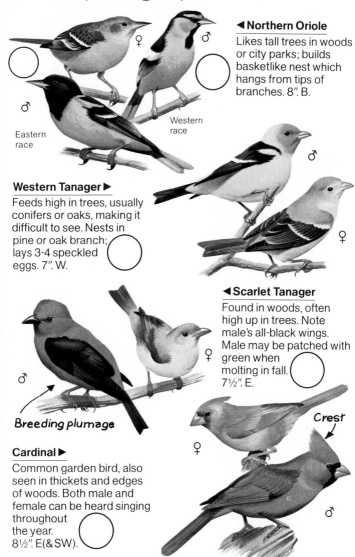

◄ Northern Oriole
Likes tall trees in woods or city parks; builds basketlike nest which hangs from tips of branches. 8″. B.

Eastern race

Western race

Western Tanager ►
Feeds high in trees, usually conifers or oaks, making it difficult to see. Nests in pine or oak branch; lays 3-4 speckled eggs. 7″. W.

◄ Scarlet Tanager
Found in woods, often high up in trees. Note male's all-black wings. Male may be patched with green when molting in fall. 7½″. E.

Breeding plumage

Cardinal ►
Common garden bird, also seen in thickets and edges of woods. Both male and female can be heard singing throughout the year. 8½″. E(&SW).

Crest

Grosbeaks, Buntings, Finch

Rose-breasted Grosbeak ▶

Found in woods, orchards and gardens. Male has rosy patch under wing which shows in flight. Nest is placed on a low branch. 8". E.

Yellow underwings show in flight

◀ Evening Grosbeak

Nests in conifers. May be seen at garden feeders in winter; is very fond of sunflower seeds. Notice its very large bill. 8". B.

Indigo Bunting ▶

Seen in hedges and near woods. Nests in bushes. 5½". E.

Lazuli Bunting ▶

Male often sings from a tree or telephone wire. 5½". W.

Lazuli Bunting

Indigo Bunting

◀ House Finch

Found in brush, desert, orchards and suburbs in West; cities, particularly New York, in East. Nests in bushes or on buildings. 5½". B(W).

Finches, Dickcissel, Towhee

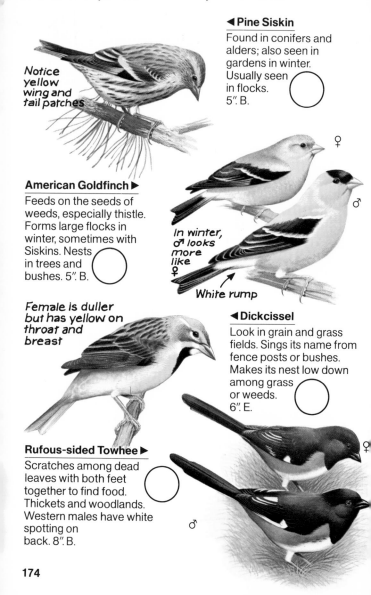

Notice yellow wing and tail patches

◄ Pine Siskin
Found in conifers and alders; also seen in gardens in winter. Usually seen in flocks. 5″. B.

American Goldfinch ►
Feeds on the seeds of weeds, especially thistle. Forms large flocks in winter, sometimes with Siskins. Nests in trees and bushes. 5″. B.

In winter, ♂ looks more like ♀

White rump

♀

♂

Female is duller but has yellow on throat and breast

◄ Dickcissel
Look in grain and grass fields. Sings its name from fence posts or bushes. Makes its nest low down among grass or weeds. 6″. E.

Rufous-sided Towhee ►
Scratches among dead leaves with both feet together to find food. Thickets and woodlands. Western males have white spotting on back. 8″. B.

♀

♂

Junco, Sparrows

Dark-eyed Junco ▶

Seen in coniferous forests in summer; visits fields and gardens in winter. Western "Oregon" race (not shown) has black hood, chestnut back. 6". B.

Eastern "slate-colored" race

Female has no black "bib"

♂

◀ House Sparrow

European bird, introduced to New York in 1850; now very common in cities and farmland throughout North America. Not a true sparrow. Untidy nest. 6". B.

Tree Sparrow ▶

Breeds in far north; in winter visits willow and birch scrub, fields and thickets. Can be seen in flocks, making "tinkling" sound. 6". B.

Notice dark spot on breast

◀ Chipping Sparrow

Common in gardens and parks, where it often feeds on lawns. Nests in dense shrubbery and lines its nest with animal hair. 5½". B.

Sparrows

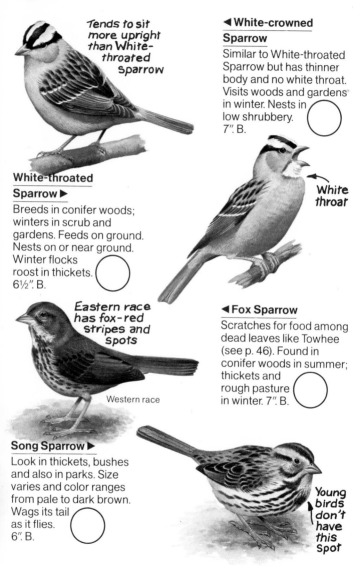

Tends to sit more upright than White-throated sparrow

White-throated Sparrow ►

Breeds in conifer woods; winters in scrub and gardens. Feeds on ground. Nests on or near ground. Winter flocks roost in thickets. 6½". B.

◄ **White-crowned Sparrow**

Similar to White-throated Sparrow but has thinner body and no white throat. Visits woods and gardens in winter. Nests in low shrubbery. 7". B.

White throat

Eastern race has fox-red stripes and spots

Western race

◄ **Fox Sparrow**

Scratches for food among dead leaves like Towhee (see p. 46). Found in conifer woods in summer; thickets and rough pasture in winter. 7". B.

Song Sparrow ►

Look in thickets, bushes and also in parks. Size varies and color ranges from pale to dark brown. Wags its tail as it flies. 6". B.

Young birds don't have this spot

Hints on birdwatching

Why watch birds? Birds are everywhere at all seasons of the year, which makes watching them a good hobby. It is easy to start – just look out your window. No great skill or knowledge is needed and there is no limit to what you can learn. You probably already know some birds: Robin, Jay, Pigeon, Crow, House Sparrow, Starling, Swallow and Cardinal.

Wherever you live you can see birds all year. But you will see the greatest number and variety of birds during the spring and fall. This is when the birds migrate; that is, they move from one place to another. Depending on where you live, spring migration can start as early as March and end as late as May; fall migration starts, some places, as early as the end of August and goes on until November. Some birds migrate early, others later; still others (like the Cardinal) do not migrate at all.

Identifying birds
The best way to start birdwatching is to learn to identify the birds you see. When out birding, keep your binoculars handy. Learn to focus them quickly, while keeping your eye on the bird.

Ask yourself these questions when you see a bird:

Where did you see it? Where the bird is found (its *habitat*) is one step in identification. Birds may be grouped according to where they live: herons are found on beaches or in marshes; Bobwhites in fields; and warblers in trees or bushes. You won't see a Pheasant in the water or a Canada Goose on a tree.

Then notice the *way it flies*. Does it fly in a straight line? Does it glide, bounce or hover?

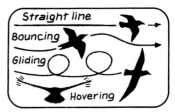

Next look at the *color* of the bird's feathers. Are there any special *markings,* such as wingbars, collars or eye stripes? Is the *breast* white, spotted, streaked, or barred?

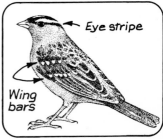

What *shape* is the bird, and what shape is its tail? How does the bird *swim, perch* or *stand*? What is the bird's *size*? Is it as big as a Crow? a Robin? a Sparrow?

Different birds have different *songs or calls*. Song is another means of identifying birds, but this is difficult, and songs are hard to describe. There are a few songs, though, that are easy. These songs are the name of the bird, like To-whee and Bob-white. Birds use song in courtship and also to defend their nesting territory.

Nests

Birds' nests are made of a great variety of materials and are found in many places: on sand dunes (Black Skimmers), on cliffs (Razorbills), under overhangs or eaves (Barn Swallows), and in holes in trees. Some birds are called colonial birds. They nest very close together (egrets, herons, and terns). Some birds make no nests at all (Whip-poor-wills).

Most small birds, like warblers, and finches, build small cuplike nests. They use grasses and sometimes animal hair.

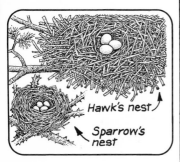

Hawk's nest

Sparrow's nest

Larger birds, like hawks and owls, build their nests with large sticks. Sometimes they use an old nest. With experience, you will be able to identify birds' nests, too. If you get too close to a bird's nest you might harm the bird. That is not what you mean to do, but it is often the result. Some birds will chase you away; terns and gulls will dive at you. But others may get frightened and leave the nest. So it is *very* important *never* to approach a nest too closely or to touch the bird's eggs. For birds that nest on the ground the danger is even greater – you might step in the nest by mistake. It is *illegal* to disturb nesting birds or their eggs. The best thing to do is to leave nesting birds alone. Birdwatch from a distance; use your binoculars.

Fascinating facts

Even though there seems to be a lot to look for in birding, don't get discouraged because it is really very easy. And birds are fascinating creatures. They change their feathers (molt) every year. Some birds, like goldfinches, have special feathers for the breeding season only. Owls have such terrific hearing that they hear their prey rather than see it – after all, they hunt at night. And Arctic Terns fly around the globe, from Alaska to Antarctica every year. Wading birds have webbed feet so they can walk on marshy ground, while perching birds (like finches) have feet that lock around a branch or wire to keep them from falling off (see picture).

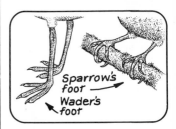

Sparrow's foot

Wader's foot

Things to remember

There are a few things to be careful about when you go birdwatching. It is not a good idea to go off by yourself unless you know the area you are hiking. There is a chance of hurting your feet in rocky country, of spraining your ankle in a boggy marsh, or of getting lost in the woods. Learn to recognize poison ivy and poison oak. Be aware of snakes and other wildlife in the area where you are walking. Remember: it is their home – you are a visitor.

Identifying shapes

One of the ways you can learn to recognize different birds is by their shape, which is often very distinctive. See if you can identify the birds shown on this page. The answers are below.

1. Mallard 2. Loon 3. Red-tailed Hawk
4. Bobwhite 5. Snowy Egret 6. Belted Kingfisher
7. Herring Gull 8. Common Flicker
9. Mockingbird 10. Barn Swallow
11. American Robin 12. Cardinal 13. Starling
14. White-breasted Nuthatch

Making a suet feeder

Insect-eating birds, such as woodpeckers, prefer suet to seed. Other birds, too, need suet to supplement their diet. If you have a suet feeder in addition to a bird table, you will attract a wide variety of birds to your yard. You can get suet from your butcher or from the meat counter at your supermarket.

Fill your suet feeder regularly. You can make or buy suet seed cakes, or just stuff chunks of plain suet into the feeder.

Here is how to make a simple suet feeder that will attach to a tree trunk.

You will need:
1. A piece of ¾"-thick plywood, 8" x 4".
2. A wood preservative (stain or varnish) and a paintbrush.
3. A piece of wire mesh, 8" square, with ½" openings.
4. 9 staple nails and a hammer.
5. A screw eye and a 1½"-long nail.

1

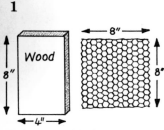

Stain or varnish the wood on all sides. Let it dry for 24 hours.

2

Bend the mesh around the wood to form a type of envelope or thin basket. The wire should be about 1" away from the wood.

3

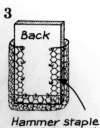

Turn the wood over and nail down the mesh, using the staple nails. Use three nails on each side.

4

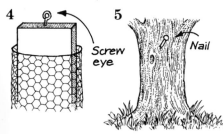

Screw the screw eye onto the top of the feeder.

5

Hammer the 1½" nail into a tree trunk, at a slight angle. Hang your feeder.

Backyard bird survey

Why not keep a record of the birds that visit your yard? The more feeders and different types of food you have, the more species of birds you'll attract. It is good to know what certain birds like to eat. Here is a list of some birds and the foods they like.

Birds	Food
Cardinal, Pine Siskin, Junco, Titmouse, Nuthatches, Finches, Chickadee, Grosbeaks, Jays, Sparrows, Doves, Crossbills	Sunflower seed
Pheasant, Chickadee, Cardinal, Titmouse, Jays, Doves	Cracked corn
Goldfinch, Chickadee, Pine Siskin	Thistle seed
Mockingbird, Catbird	Raisins
Robin, Mockingbird, Wrens	Apple pieces
Woodpeckers, Wrens, Chickadee, Nuthatches, Starling, Finches, Brown Creeper, Titmouse	Suet

It is also very important to have water for the birds. A simple birdbath (not too deep) will do. Put it in a sunny spot. Because birds have no teeth, they need to eat grit. The grit helps them to digest (grind up) their food. If you have a bird table, you might set one corner aside for grit. Birds also like the berries of certain trees and shrubs.

The chart below is an example of a backyard survey. Perhaps you'd like to keep one like this.

NAMES OF BIRDS SEEN	MONTH WHEN SEEN J F M A M J J A S O N D	FOODS EATEN	BATHE	DRINK	WHERE THEY NEST
Chickadee	✓✓✓✓✓✓✓✓✓✓	Suet, sun-flower seed	✓	✓	In bird house.
Robin	✓✓✓✓✓✓✓	worms		✓	Don't know.
Red-winged blackbird	✓✓✓ ✓✓	mixed bird seed	✓	✓	Don't know.
House sparrow	✓✓✓✓✓✓✓✓✓✓✓✓	mixed seed, sunflower seed	✓	✓	Under porch eaves.

Organizations you can join

As a birdwatcher, you may want to join a conservation or birding society. Many of them sponsor trips and educational or interpretive programs. Some maintain sanctuaries and nature centers. A few of the major North American organizations are listed here:

American Birding Association, Box 4335, Austin, TX 78765.
*National Audubon Society, 950 Third Avenue, New York, NY 10022.
National Wildlife Federation, 1412 16 Street NW, Washington, DC 20036.
*The Nature Conservancy, National Office, 1800 N. Kent Street, Arlington, VA 22209.

*Sierra Club, National Office, 1050 Mills Tower, San Fransisco, CA 94104.
Canadian Nature Federation, 46 Elgin Street, Ottowa, Ontario K1P 5K6.
Long Point Bird Observatory, Box 160, Port Rowan, Ontario NOE 1MO.

*These organizations have local chapters. There may be one where you live. To find out, write them at the above address or ask at your public library. In addition, there might be a local bird club or nature group that you could join.

Books to read

Birds of North America; a Guide to Field Identification. Robbins, Bruun, and Zim (Golden/paperback). Uses color pictures and range maps.
A Field Guide to Birds. Roger Tory Peterson (Houghton Mifflin/paperback). In two volumes, eastern and western. Most pictures in color. There is a special guide for Texas and nearby states.
The Audubon Society Field Guide to North American Birds. (Knopf). In two volumes, eastern and western. Has color photos.
Watching Birds; an Introduction to Ornithology. Roger Tory Peterson (Houghton Mifflin).
The Birdwatcher's Bible. George Laycock (Doubleday/paperback). Tells you about birds and birding.

A Birdwatcher's Guide to the Eastern United States. Alice Geffen (Barron's/paperback). Describes over 700 places to go birding east of the Mississippi River.
The Habitat Guide to Birding. Thomas McElroy, Jr. (Knopf). Tells you how to find certain birds according to where they live.
How to Attract, House and Feed Birds. Walter Shutz (Collier/paperback). Gives plans for building bird houses and feeders.
1001 Questions Answered About Birds. Allan and Helen Cruickshank. (Dover/paperback). Full of information and fun.
Birds in Peril. John Mackenzie (Houghton Mifflin). A guide to endangered bird species in North America.

Scorecard

When you have seen and identified a bird, use this scorecard to look up the number of points you have scored.

Before looking up your score, look at the map below, where you will see that North America has been divided into two main regions—Eastern and Western; the Eastern region is the area east of the Rocky Mountains, and the Western region is the remaining area, including the Rocky Mountains. The line running from San Francisco in the West across to Washington D.C. in the East shows the dividing line between North and South, as defined in this book.

There is a separate scorecard for each region, and the birds found in each are arranged in alphabetical order.

A low score means that the bird is common and quite often seen; the highest score is 25, and the higher the score, the rarer the bird. Some birds, like the Crow, are very common throughout North America and therefore have a score of 5 for both regions. Others may be fairly rare in one area and not seen at all in the other (the Orchard Oriole scores 20 in the East but is not found at all in the West).

When you have found your score, you can either ring it in pencil in the book, or you can keep a record of your score in a notebook. Either way you can add up your total score whenever you like.

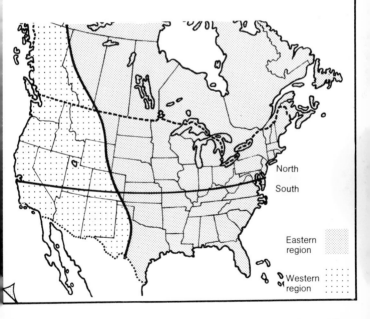

North
South

Eastern region

Western region

Western Region

	Score		Score		Score
Auklet, Cassin's	20	Dowitcher, Short-billed	20	Hawk, Sharp-shinned	15
Avocet, American	15	Duck, Ruddy	15	Heron, Black-crowned Night	15
Blackbird, Red-winged	5	Duck, Wood	20	Heron, Great Blue	10
Bluebird, Mountain	15	Dunlin	10	Heron, Green	15
Bluebird, Western	15	Eagle, Bald	25	Hummingbird, Black-chinned	15
Bobolink	20	Egrets, Great and Snowy	10	Hummingbird, Rufous	15
Bobwhite	10	Finch, House	5	Jaeger, Parasitic	20
Bufflehead	15	Flicker, Common	10	Jay, Steller's	10
Bunting, Lazuli	15	Flycatcher, Willow/Alder	15	Junco, Dark-eyed	5
Canvasback	15	Gallinule, Common	15	Kestrel, American	10
Cardinal	15	Godwit, Marbled	15	Killdeer	10
Catbird, Gray	10	Goldfinch, American	10	Kingbird, Eastern	15
Chickadee, Black-capped	5	Goose, Canada	5	Kingbird, Western	10
Coot, American	5	Goose, Snow/Blue	15	Kingfisher, Belted	10
Cormorant, Double-crested	5	Goose, White-fronted	15	Kinglet, Golden-crowned	10
Cowbird, Brown-headed	10	Grebe, Pied-billed	10	Lark, Horned	15
Crane, Sandhill	15	Grosbeak, Evening	10	Loon, Common	15
Creeper, Brown	10	Grouse, Ruffed	15	Magpie, Black-billed	10
Crow, Common	5	Grouse, Spruce	20	Magpie, Yellow-billed	15
Cuckoo, Yellow-billed	15	Gull, Herring	5	Mallard	5
Dipper	15	Gull, Ring-billed	10	Martin, Purple	10
Dove, Mourning	5	Hawk, Marsh	15	Meadowlark, Eastern	20
Dove, Rock	5	Hawk, Red-tailed	15	Meadowlark, Western	10

	Score		Score		Score
Merganser, Red-breasted	15	Robin, American	5	Tern, Royal	20
Mockingbird	15	Sanderling	10	Thrush, Hermit	10
Murre, Common	N20 S25	Sandpipers, Least and Spotted	10	Towhee, Rufous-sided	10
Murre, Thick-billed	20	Sapsucker, Yellow-bellied	15	Turnstone, Ruddy	15
Nighthawk, Common	15	Scaup, Lesser	10	Veery	15
Nuthatch, Red-breasted	15	Shoveler, Northern	10	Vireos, Red-eyed and Solitary	10
Nuthatch, White-breasted	10	Siskin, Pine	10	Vulture, Black	15
Oriole, Northern	15	Snipe, Common	15	Vulture, Turkey	10
Osprey	20	Sora	20	Warbler, Black-and-white	10
Owl, Great Horned	20	Sparrow, Chipping	10	Warbler, Wilson's	10
Owl, Saw-whet	20	Sparrow, Fox	10	Warbler, Yellow	10
Owl, Screech	20	Sparrow, House	5	Warbler, Yellow-rumped	10
Pelican, Brown	20	Sparrow, Song	10	Waterthrush, Northern	10
Phalarope, Northern	20	Sparrow, Tree	10	Waxwing, Cedar	15
Pheasant, Ring-necked	10	Sparrow, White-crowned	5	Whimbrel	20
Pigeon, Band-tailed	15	Sparrow, White-throated	5	Whip-poor-will	15
Pintail	10	Starling	5	Wigeon, American	15
Plover, Black-bellied	15	Stilt, Black-necked	10	Willet	10
Plover, Semipalmated	10	Swallow, Bank	10	Woodpecker, Downy	10
Puffin, Tufted	20	Swallows, Barn and Tree	10	Woodpecker, Hairy	5
Quail, California	10	Swan, Whistling	N10 S20	Wren, Bewick's and House	10
Rail, Virginia	20	Tanager, Western	15	Wren, Long-billed Marsh	15
Raven, Common	15	Teal, Blue-winged	10	Yellowlegs, Greater	10
Redstart, American	10	Terns, Black and Caspian	15	Yellowthroat, Common	10
Roadrunner	15	Tern, Least	15		

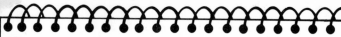

Eastern Region

	Score		Score		Score
Blackbird, Red-winged ✗	5	Duck, Black ✗	5	Grouse. Spruce	15
Bluebird, Eastern ✗	15	Duck, Ruddy ✗	15	Gull, Great Black-backed	10
Bobolink	15	Duck, Wood ✗	15	Gull, Herring ✗	5
Bobwhite ✗	10	Dunlin	10	Gull, Laughing	10
Brant	15	Eagle, Bald	25	Gull, Ring-billed	10
Bufflehead ✗	15	Egret, Great ✗	10	Hawk, Broad-winged	15
Bunting, Indigo ✗	15	Egret, Snowy	10	Hawk, Marsh	15
Canvasback ✗	15	Finch, House ✗	10	Hawk, Red-tailed ✗	15
Cardinal ✗	5	Flicker, Common ✗	10	Hawk, Sharp-shinned	15
Catbird, Gray ✗	10	Flycatcher, Great Crested	15	Heron, Black-crowned Night ✗	15
Chickadee, Black-capped ✗	5	Flycatcher, Willow/Alder	15	Heron, Great Blue ✗	10
Coot, American ✗	5	Gallinule, Common	10	Heron, Green	15
Cormorant, Double-crested	10	Gannet	20	Hummingbird, Ruby-throated ✗	15
Cowbird, Brown-headed	10	Godwit, Marbled	25	Ibis, Glossy	15
Crane, Sandhill ✗	20	Goldfinch, American ✗	10	Jaeger, Parasitic	20
Creeper, Brown	15	Goose, Canada ✗	5	Jay, Blue ✗	5
Crow, Common ✗	5	Goose, Snow/Blue ✗	15	Junco, Dark-eyed ✗	5
Cuckoo, Black-billed	15	Goose, White-fronted	20	Kestrel, American	10
Cuckoo, Yellow-billed	15	Grackle, Common ✗	5	Killdeer ✗	10
Dickcissel	15	Grebe, Pied-billed ✗	10	Kingbird, Eastern	15
Dove, Mourning ✗	5	Grosbeak, Evening ✗	10	Kingbird, Western	20
Dove, Rock	5	Grosbeak, Rose-breasted ✗	15	Kingfisher, Belted ✗	10
Dowitcher, Short-billed	15	Grouse, Ruffed ✗	N15 S25	Kinglet, Golden-crowned	10

	Score		Score		Score
Lark, Horned	15	Pheasant, Ring-necked	10	Sparrow, Song	10
Loon, Common	15	Phoebe, Eastern	10	Sparrow, Tree	10
Magpie, Black-billed	10	Pintail	15	Sparrow, White-crowned	10
Mallard	5	Plover, Black-bellied	15	Sparrow, White-throated	5
Martin, Purple	10	Plover, Semipalmated	10	Starling	5
Meadowlark, Eastern	10	Puffin, Common	25	Swallow, Bank	10
Meadowlark, Western	20	Rail, Virginia	20	Swallow, Barn	10
Merganser, Red-breasted	15	Raven, Common	20	Swallow, Tree	5
Mockingbird	10	Razorbill	20	Swan, Whistling	N15 S20
Murre, Common	20	Redstart, American	10	Swift, Chimney	10
Murre, Thick-billed	20	Robin, American	5	Tanager, Scarlet	15
Nighthawk, Common	15	Sanderling	10	Teal, Blue-winged	10
Nuthatch, Red-breasted	15	Sandpiper, Least	10	Tern, Black	15
Nuthatch, White-breasted	10	Sandpiper, Semipalmated	10	Tern, Caspian	15
Oriole, Northern	15	Sandpiper, Spotted	10	Tern, Common	10
Oriole, Orchard	20	Sapsucker, Yellow-bellied	15	Tern, Least	15
Osprey	20	Scaup, Lesser	10	Tern, Royal	15
Owl, Barred	20	Shoveler, Northern	10	Thrasher, Brown	10
Owl, Great Horned	20	Siskin, Pine	10	Thrush, Hermit	10
Owl, Saw-whet	20	Skimmer, Black	15	Thrush, Wood	10
Owl, Screech	20	Snipe, Common	15	Titmouse, Tufted	10
Parula, Northern	15	Sora	20	Towhee, Rufous-sided	10
Pelican, Brown	15	Sparrow, Chipping	10	Turkey	N20 S15
Pewee, Eastern Wood	10	Sparrow, Fox	10	Turnstone, Ruddy	15
Phalarope, Northern	20	Sparrow, House	5	Veery	10

	Score		Score		Score
Vireo, Red-eyed	10				
Vireo, Solitary	10				
Vulture, Turkey	10				
Warbler, Black-and-white	10				
Warbler, Chestnut-sided	15				
Warbler, Magnolia	15				
Warbler, Wilson's	15				
Warbler, Yellow	10				
Warbler, Yellow-rumped	10				
Waterthrush, Northern	10				
Waxwing, Cedar ✕	15				
Whimbrel	20				
Whip-poor-will ✕	15				
Wigeon, American ✕	15				
Willet	10				
Woodcock, American ✕	15				
Woodpecker, Downy ✕	5				
Woodpecker, Hairy ✕	5				
Woodpecker, Red-bellied	10				
Wren, Bewick's	15				
Wren, House ✕	10				
Wren, Long-billed Marsh	15				
Yellowlegs, Greater	10				
Yellowthroat, Common	10				

Glossary

Breeding plumage - the feathers during the time of mating, nesting and laying eggs.

Camouflage - when the color of a bird matches its background and makes it difficult to see.

Colony - group of birds of the same species nesting together.

Conifer (Coniferous) - trees that bear cones, have needlelike leaves and are usually evergreen. Pines and firs are typical conifers.

Deciduous - a tree, or any sort of plant, that loses its leaves every year, usually in the fall.

Courtship display - when a male bird attracts a mate. Some birds show off their plumage; others put on a **display** in the air.

Cover - places where birds hide, such as thickets, bushes or thick grass.

Habitat - the particular type of place where a bird lives.

Migration - the movement of birds from one place to another, usually from their breeding area to one where they spend the winter. A migrating bird is called a migrant, or visitor.

Molt - when birds shed their old feathers and grow new ones. All birds do this at least once a year. In ducks, the duller plumage that remains is called **eclipse plumage.**

Palmated - refers to a bird's feet, when they are divided like the fingers of a hand.

Phase - one of several different plumages that a particular bird has e.g. the Screech Owl.

Race - a subspecies; a geographical group of birds that is slightly different from another geographical group within the same species.

Roost - to settle in one place for the night. A roost is the name given to a place where birds sleep.

Species - a group of birds that all look alike and behave in the same way e.g. Herring Gull is the name of one species.

Speculum - a patch of color on a bird's wing, particularly among ducks.

Index

Part 1 – Wild flowers

Part 2 – Trees

If a tree has another common
name which is also widely
used, this is shown below in
parentheses.

Part 3 – Birds